P

EDUCATI

John Vaizey is Professor of Economics at Brunel, a new university in London. Born in 1929, he was educated at elementary, special and grammar schools, was a scholar of Queens' College, Cambridge, and took a 'First' in economics. He became a Fellow of St Catharine's College, Cambridge, and later worked for a while at London University. He then became Fellow and Tutor in economics at Worcester College, Oxford. He has many official duties. He has worked in international organizations – notably U.N.E.S.C.O. and O.E.C.D. – has travelled widely and is a frequent broadcaster and lecturer, especially in the U.S.A. He is married to an American and has three children, two of whom attend the local (racially mixed) primary school. The third is too young for school. Among his other books are *The Costs of Education*, *The Economics of Education*, *Scenes from Institutional Life*, *Barometer Man*, *Education in the Modern World*, *Capitalism* and *The Sleepless Lunch*.

DISPOSED OF
BY LIBRARY
HOUSE OF LORDS

JOHN VAIZEY

Education for Tomorrow

PENGUIN BOOKS

Penguin Books Ltd, Harmondsworth, Middlesex, England
Penguin Books Inc., 7110 Ambassador Road, Baltimore, Maryland 21207, U.S.A.
Penguin Books Australia Ltd, Ringwood, Victoria, Australia

—

First published as a Penguin Special 1962
Revised and reprinted in Pelican Books 1966, 1967, 1970, 1971

—

Copyright © John Vaizey, 1962, 1966, 1970

—

Made and printed in Great Britain
by Hazell Watson & Viney Ltd
Aylesbury, Bucks
Set in Linotype Juliana

CONTENTS

In memory of Hugh and Ruth

INTRODUCTION

THIS book is a survey of the state of education in Britain two-thirds of the way through the twentieth century, with an attempt to take a forward look. It draws upon a number of disciplines – history, economics, public administration, social administration, sociology and psychology – in only limited areas of which can I authoritatively claim expertise. I am grateful to my friends and colleagues who have guided me through the territories with which I am professionally less familiar.

In 1961 I wrote a short paperback called *Education for Tomorrow*, in a series entitled 'Britain in the Sixties'. It came out in 1962, and it was then out of print almost from its publication. The fact that a 'popular' book on education sold out at once was indicative, at that time, of an extraordinary change in the public standing of education. People were concerned about it to a degree that had never been known before. In this present book, which might perhaps be called 'Britain in the Seventies', we can to some extent take the enthusiasm for granted. Therefore, this book, though it incorporates parts of the other book which are of more permanent interest, has completely new chapters dealing with matters where the situation has changed beyond all recognition.

Despite the urgency of the needs in education, and the apparent insolubility of the problems that arose (like the shortage of teachers), the problems of the 1970s are of a different order from those of the 1960s. Perhaps the biggest surprise of all is the extent that the things that I wrote eight years ago, in a visionary mood as it were, are now accepted as commonplace. The distinction, for instance, between the 'strong' and the 'weak' definition of equality of opportunity which Mr Anthony Crosland drew at a Fabian Easter School I chaired in 1960 was used three years later in the introduction of the Newsom Report. The plea for higher education to be regarded as a system anticipated the Robbins Report. There is cause to be hopeful, therefore, even when problems seem insoluble.

London, January 1970   J.V.

CHAPTER ONE

THE IMPORTANCE OF EDUCATION

I WILL begin by describing the scope of this book. It is concerned chiefly with the shape of the education system in Britain, and how one thinks that shape will change over the next ten years or so. But in describing the education system we have also to describe the inwardness of the schools and colleges: what the teachers try to do and what the pupils are learning, and why they do it. We cannot avoid, that is, a philosophy of education. Mine is a pragmatic one. We will look at what the schools are doing before we suggest what they ought to do. And when I suggest what they ought to do I will do so on the basis of some fairly clearly defined criteria.

The word 'education' is given many interpretations, and indeed it is a very loose concept covering a variety of contradictory ideas: it concerns hundreds of thousands of teachers and millions of children of all sorts and conditions.

Any generalization about this complex situation is bound to be misleading. And we need a proper humility about what 'education' can do. For one thing, not all teachers and pupils will have the same objectives. For another, the part that formal schooling plays in society, its effects on values and on material development, is little understood. Probably its effects are small compared with the effects of ordinary family life, or even of advertising. Put modestly, what we can say about schools and universities is that they exert an influence on us, both as individuals and as a nation; and the economic and social conditions in this country are now ripe for a big push forward. Even to put it at its barest minimum, we are a wealthy society which can afford to give all children and young people the opportunity to stay off the labour market and off the streets; and we can spare enough adults to work with them. But a stronger case for spending more on education can be found in the reasons why we are wealthy; ours is an affluent society because our knowledge of the physical and social world is expanding at a fantastic rate. Just to keep abreast of this expansion, to run the economy and the society that it permits, means that people have to know far more than ever before and to be far more flexible, adaptable, and resilient to change.

Education is not all-important; but it is, I think, much more important than it was, because it occupies a far greater part of an individual's life than ever before, and because without it more and more people could not earn their living. It enables them to enjoy modern life and to make more of it. It has become, too, an avenue of social promotion which has now overtaken such things as success in small business or a 'successful' marriage – it has become virtually *the* avenue for social mobility. Finally, and most important, parents now care about it far more than they ever did. If we are sensible we can take this care for education and use it to make Britain more go-ahead and a better place to live in.

Schools both affect and mirror the quality of society. Take the growth in the strength of family life, for instance. The serious-minded husband and wife, buying their house on a mortgage, rearing the well-dressed children you see all over the country, are deeply concerned that their children shall get a good start in life. Of course one can sneer at this : 'Keeping up with the Joneses', 'Death in a suburb', and so on. But compared with life in the Orwellian slums of the thirties, or the Wellsian small-shopkeeper existence in Edwardian days, this new way of living (new only in that it is *the* typical way of life) is in almost every way better.

So far all the majority of parents have said is that they want more education. Their demands are simple : that their children should speak 'nicely', learn good manners, get a 'qualification'. They hope that the children will get on in the world and get 'good' jobs. But there is a second stage of enthusiasm – what should education be about? And in this the 'new' classes have not yet reached the certainties of the old professional classes, who have long been sure of what they wanted from schools and on the whole have satisfied their needs.

This stage is now upon us in State education. The debate is growing among parents, teachers, and pupils about the techniques of teaching; about the curriculum; about boarding schools and day schools; about the relationship between work, play, and school. These are all subjects which were neglected while the prime necessity was to provide enough schools which were not blackboard jungles and where the lavatories flushed. The debate must be welcomed – even though it means change everywhere. Indeed, we must get used to living with change, and not expect ever to achieve an equilibrium where all is calm.

As people and their ideas become adapted to the new ways of life, so will the schools; they in their turn will be one of the chief agencies through which change will be brought about, and this in turn will affect the economy of the whole country.

For modern education affects the economy in a number of ways; not only does it increase the flow of skills, but it assists people to acquire new techniques. Moreover, it tends to destroy the traditional attitudes which so impeded progress, and it links knowledge with methods of production. The economy in turn reacts on the educational system through science, which has now grown more important in industry and so is increasingly taught in school. As traditional crafts have died out, so people have had to be taught sufficient basic knowledge to enable them to learn modern production methods and how to adapt themselves to all the changing techniques which appear during their adult lives.

On the one hand, therefore, education helps to strengthen the economy, for it is an investment in manpower; on the other hand, it is very expensive. As the national income grows so more can be spared for education : its share grew from one per cent in 1900 to five and a half per cent now, and it ought to be eight per cent by 1980. Even then, our economy is moving more slowly than that of some of our European neighbours, because we are shorter of engineers and scientists than they are. We are insufficiently alert to the outside world. Our export drive is weakened because we have not enough salesmen who can speak Spanish or Swedish : German salesmen can vaunt their wares in every language. We need hundreds of thousands more qualified people very quickly, if our country is to be serviced and made to pay its way. The Russians, the Americans and the French have realized this. Have we? The omens are still not good.

Education is important, therefore, not only to help our children, to give them better lives, to improve the society in which we live, to enable this country to go forward paying its way and competing internationally; but it is essential if we are to survive in a changing, technical and scientific age. But quantity of education by itself is not enough. What also matters is the kind and type; it must be geared to the world we live in, prepare people for life and for change, help them to develop and to become adaptable, and it must reach them all.

Our education system is too often inefficient, divided, and unnecessarily selective. The number of children is increasing, and yet classrooms are already overcrowded. Insufficient teachers and too few scientists means that we need to fill the gap by more higher education for greater numbers. Consequently there is a dual problem : to provide enough education, and to improve it at the same time.

We would be wise to remember how much education *has* improved, and how much better it has become almost year in and year out ever since the oldest can remember. Despite the gloomy prophets, more has not meant worse so far.

Let it not be thought, however, that concern with numbers

and with 'improvement', concern with the economic and social aspects of education, means that one thinks of education wholly in those terms. School and college mean so much to so many – friends, ideas, happiness and unhappiness – that only very concrete writing can tell us much about what it is really like to be 'educated'. The provision of schools and colleges is a precondition of education; on the basis of our own experience and what others tell us, we can judge what we would like to happen in the schools, but the most that we may indisputably assert is that for anything to happen at all (whether we think it good or bad) we need to have schools and teachers – and the wherewithal to pay for them.

In this book I shall briefly examine our educational system as a whole according to the needs of today and with an eye to the future, in the light of modern knowledge and research, and then see how we can improve the system. We must consider those we shall be educating, who will teach them, what sort of schools we need, who will administer them, and how we can pay for it all.

The next few years, therefore, should see a continuation of the expansion in our educational programme, demanded by our new economic and social forces. Our first question is, what sort of children will our teachers have to teach?

CHAPTER TWO

EQUALITY AND ABILITY

THERE is a dilemma – probably a false dilemma – facing people who run schools and colleges. Should they do most for the clever, or for the less-clever? In one sense, the answer is obvious. If you want to teach a potential nuclear physicist, or a great musician, then he will need to be taught more than most of us. And nobody would deny that on every possible ground – the furtherance of the culture, the 'needs' of the economy, what people want for themselves – those of outstanding ability should have (and in most modern societies will get) the 'best' education going. (We will discuss what 'best' is in another chapter.) On the other hand, since it is clear that clever children for the greater part teach themselves, it might be thought that the greatest effort should be given to those that do not teach themselves – effort in terms of originality of ideas about how to teach as well as effort in terms of sheer numbers of teachers. This raises, of course, the issue of equality – and the issue of ability.

Are we not at the present moment educating the most intelligent at the expense of the less able, who need more attention, better conditions and greater help just because their environment impedes their chances of expressing themselves, of acquiring new skills, and of understanding the society in which they live? Why are we doing this, and how did it come about?

In the first place because of scarcity. If teachers are scarce, if money is short – then you have to choose. And in all countries (perhaps especially in modern democracies, as well as in England in the past) 'the rich gits richer and the poor gits poorer', in the sense that those with the means and ability to benefit from education as it is at present arranged will get most out of it – a statement that is deliberately (though not wholly) tautologous.

We know that not everyone in our society is getting the best possible education to meet his needs and to develop his abilities. The debate on ability is now virtually over. Much remains to be discovered about what causes some people to be more intelligent, or more able, or to have greater application than others. Today we know far more about ability and intelligence than we did. So much more, in fact, that it is now clear that the great tradition of belief in equality of opportunity was not only correct – in that there were still great reserves of untapped ability in our society – but that it was even an understatement of what needs to be achieved if all sorts and kinds of abilities are to be developed to the full.

One of the great drives towards improvement in education has always come from the passionate concern of reformers with equality. Until recently this was defined simply as equality of opportunity – that, given the opening, those with intelligence would rise to the top. It was believed that there were many working-class boys and girls – village Hampdens – who, if offered the chance, could become great statesmen, great scientists, or great writers. It used to be thought that one or two in a thousand could be identified and rescued – the rest would be left. Scholarships were created to provide places for children of high ability, largely from the white-collar working-class. Gradually, with the growth of sophistication in genetic ideas and techniques for measuring ability, it became clear that a great deal of talent of the highest level was, in fact, lost by inegalitarian systems of education. The idea that equality of opportunity might mean opportunity to develop any abilities a child might have, even if these did not lie solely in the intellectual field, is a much more modern interpretation of this phrase. It is only recently that it has become accepted that every child is entitled to an adequate education, though at the present moment only those in the top part of the intelligence distribution gain an education which is in any respect equivalent to that provided for many middle-class children by their parents.

Yet in principle and in law every child now has the right to an education suited to his age, abilities and aptitude, and a great deal of the effort of educational psychologists is concerned with placing children in schools or in courses which appear suited to their talents. However, the process of intelligence testing – which came into the schools in America during the early years of this century – which has become more and more refined, and more and more complex, was used for twenty years or more as a major part of the process of selection. Hence intelligence testing, in itself a complex scientific activity, subject to great limitations of which psychologists are fully aware, became identified with a particular system of education – the division of the secondary schools into grammar and non-grammar schools. This division was due to complicated historical circumstances, as we shall explain later; but the use of scientifically structured tests appeared to give this historical process of selection an apparently 'objective' scientific basis. Originally this 'scientific' method of selection was based upon the assumption that it was possible to make a selection of children at a comparatively early age, which could later be justified by the achievements of these children. The more competent and distinguished scientists in this field have long known that most of these predictions were self-confirming. That is to say, a child from a good home sent to a good school was bound to seem more intelligent, and more able to benefit, from education, and so to have the chance to be better educated and to get farther ahead than a child from a poor home sent to an overcrowded elementary school. In addition, recent inquiries suggest that intelligence, in so far as it can be measured at all, is largely acquired. Marxist scholars have all along held that intelligence is entirely acquired, but Western scholars argue against this theory from their research on the similar achievements of identical twins separated at birth, and the different achievements of non-identical twins brought up together. Similar cases have suggested that there must be an inherent quality in intelligence, even if the acquired element is a large part of the whole. Nevertheless, those systems of education which, like the Russian, are based upon the assumption that all children are born equal, are probably more satisfactory in practice than those which, like our own (up to recently in the greater part of the country), have been based on the assumption that children are born – intellectually – sheep or goats.

A great deal of the debate about equality has now become out of date, since it is based upon three assumptions, none of which is any longer thought to be wholly correct. The first is that educational resources will always be scarce, so that a choice must be made between the children of any age group who should be adequately educated, and those who should receive second best. This is partly true at present. As we shall show below, the shortage of teachers is likely to last for some time. But compared with the past we are very much better off than we were, and projections of the future economic conditions of Britain make it possible that the economic problem in its present form may be solved sooner or later, as Lord Keynes said it would be.

In any case, the most pressing problems of scarcity are not ours any longer; and we are no longer faced with choosing between a good education for the few and an indifferent education for the many. Our choices are more complex and less constrained by poverty than they were.

Secondly, it has always been assumed that society depended upon the identification of some exceptional people who would later become the leaders, while the great mass would be doing routine and humdrum jobs well within the capabilities of anybody with a minimum of intelligence and training.

This is now emphatically not the case. In a modern

17

economy, jobs present a wide range of demands on talent and ability, and a highly productive society makes enormous demands upon people of all abilities, both on their general level of competence in such matters as reading, writing, calculating, driving, or managing technical equipment, and on their ability to meet the requirements of an increasingly complex social organization, while at the same time it requires a high level of emotional adjustment to situations of rapid change. Learning these techniques, abilities, and basic emotional adjustments depends to an increasing extent upon the educational system. It is becoming as important to educate the people of average and less than average ability as it is to educate the highly able. In any case, study after study has shown that unless a very wide range of ability is educated, some very able people are inevitably going to fall through the net. Even in a society such as ours, which has been organized for nearly fifty years on a basis of some equality of opportunity, two-fifths of the top ten per cent of the ability distribution still left school at sixteen in the mid-1950s.

The third assumption which is no longer thought to be true is that ability is a fixed quantum which can be identified and which to all intents and purposes remains constant throughout life. It has now been shown that the average level of ability has risen rather than fallen, if measured in terms of what the average person can do. It has been shown that children brought up in homes with satisfactory emotional adjustment, sent to good schools, staying on at school until the latest possible date, and then taking up interesting work, become more intelligent in every sense than those to whom this does not happen. In so far as there is a rise in the standard of living of the average home, an improvement in the average school, and a lengthening of school life, the number of able people will therefore multiply.

This new knowledge makes it necessary to re-examine the whole concept of 'equality of opportunity'. Mr Anthony

Crosland drew a vital distinction between the 'weak' and the 'strong' definition of equality of opportunity (a distinction that Sir Edward Boyle borrowed for his introduction to the Newsom Report). The weak definition (which had been generally accepted as the only definition up till that time) is that all children of equal (measured) ability should have roughly the same start in life. The strong definition takes account of recent psychological knowledge which points out that ability is largely acquired, and that a child can become more or less intelligent according to the kind of family he has and the social and educational experience he receives. It asserts that subject to differences in heredity and infantile experience, every child should have the same opportunity for *acquiring* measured intelligence, in so far as this can be controlled by social action.

This is clearly a revolutionary principle. It means a rapid shift towards creating a society where every child has a good home, which in turn means, as an integral part of the educational process, eliminating low incomes and bad housing, and trying to remedy the deficiencies of badly educated parents. It means sending every child to a good school. It means redefining the notion of a 'good' school. It means attempting to change the culture of whole areas. In practice it would suggest, for example, that if a boarding-school education can be given to only a small proportion of adolescents (and if it is acceptable to them) it should be given to the culturally deprived rather than to the well-endowed.

This principle underlies the Newsom Report, *Half Our Future*, which was concerned with the secondary education of the children of average and less than average ability. (It is interesting that the education of this group should have been specially referred to a committee, implying that there were special educational requirements for average children, which needed to be studied in isolation from the study of the educational needs of 'brighter' children.) The Committee found, as might have been expected, that there were significant corre-lations between social origins and academic attainment and, consequently, if anything is to be done markedly to improve the attainment of the average working-class child, a signifi-cant attempt to raise the whole environmental level in which he finds himself has to be made.

As the policy for 'culturally-deprived' areas – the Com-munity Development Areas – shows, it is impossible to con-sider the educational problems of any relatively deprived group in isolation from the social context of their deprivation. If the working class were dyed blue, the social isolation of large groups of working class children would be as visible as the social segregation of the present coloured minority; of course, the rate of assimilation of the working class is – his-torically speaking – remarkably rapid, for when you think of the comparatively recent past, it is surprising that the degree of social handicap is not greater than it is. It was estimated in 1937, for instance, that one-third of the nation's children were clinically undernourished. These children are the parents of the children now at school. Widespread poverty is as recent as that. Bad housing is, of course, still widespread. When people talk of working-class affluence they forget how recent and how – for some – superficial it is.

The question immediately arises, then, whether social change should precede educational change, or vice versa. The correct answer here is surely that they must go hand in hand. By improving housing (millions still live in houses that are overcrowded), leisure opportunities, and working conditions, we make the teacher's job easier; and by improving education we help to create the climate for every other kind of social change.

But let us now turn back for a moment to the present, and see who is being fully educated today and how far we are from attaining even the 'weak' principle that all people of equal ability should have an equal chance. In the mid nineteen fifties two-fifths of the top ten per cent of boys (measured by ability) left school at sixteen; two-thirds of the *next* twenty per cent of ability left at fifteen. On the top group at age eleven, sixty-six per cent came from the working class; forty-seven per cent of those who were in the top group at age fifteen were from the working class, and only thirty-six per cent of university entrants *from grammar schools* came from this class. (This figure would have been only about twenty to twenty-five per cent if public-school entrants had been counted.) In other words, a working-class boy (in the mid nineteen-fifties) had only a third of the chance of going to a university compared with his middle-class counterpart: contrast this with those whose parents can afford to send them to a public school, and the chances of the averagely gifted child are seen to be ludicrously small – perhaps one in fifty compared with one in five. Even to equalize opportunity on the 'weak' definition will therefore require a tremendous effort.

Those figures were taken from the Crowther Report 15–18, on the education of the adolescents. The Robbins Report on *Higher Education*, published four years later, contains material no less striking. It shows, for example (Robbins Report, p. 50), that of children born in 1940–41, 45 per cent of the children of fathers who followed higher professional occupations (doctors, lawyers, top civil servants, etc.) went to some kind of university, college or other institution of higher education, whereas only 2 per cent of the children of fathers with semi-skilled and unskilled jobs did so. Yet there were nine times as many children in the latter – the working-class group – as in the former – the higher professional group. The Report says that 'the underlying reasons for this are complex, but differences of income and of the parents' educational level and attitudes are certainly among them. The link is even more marked for girls than for boys.'

The Robbins Report goes on to show that of the boys and

girls born in 1940–41, 43 per cent of those whose fathers completed their education at the age of 18 or over, went on to higher education, but only 5 per cent of those whose fathers left school below the age of 16.

The Report draws two conclusions from its analysis – one of the most thorough pieces of work that there has ever been on the question of ability and social origin. It shows that even at present many boys and girls with the ability to do well in higher education leave school early; and that these children are to be found in all social groups though numerically, of course, the great majority are in the working class (two-thirds of the population is working class, if that class is defined as the skilled, semi-skilled and unskilled manual workers and their families). Further, talent appears to manifest itself as the opportunity to exercise it grows.

But suppose we do end up with a society from which greatly increased talent emerges? Will the clever, chosen almost at birth, use their intellectual powers for government, and create a meritocracy? Will they feel a divine right to do so, stronger even than that of the hereditary aristocracy – about whom there was at least never any damned nonsense about merit?

The danger of a meritocracy occurring is a remote one. The fear of it ignores the fact that we are at least two generations away from an approximation to equal opportunity in Mr Crosland's 'weak' sense. It ignores the fact that even in America, with a lavish education system and a democratic social structure, a high proportion of the most able people – the top one per cent – still do not go to college. It ignores the existence of Mr Crosland's revolutionary 'strong' principle of equality of opportunity, which suggests that a great proportion of society is capable of radical improvement and so, by dilution, would ultimately mitigate the more questionable aspects of a meritocracy. It postulates a division of education (and social function) along a rigid line which certainly will not accord with the probable job structure of the last quarter of this century.

There are two implicit assumptions in the minds of those who fear a meritocracy. One is that people should only be educated if there are jobs of the 'equivalent' level to go to. That begs a lot of questions, both about jobs and about schools! Many jobs now done by graduates – teaching, for example – used not to be; and should not schools be concerned in some sense with 'the whole man' (to use a rather nauseating phrase open to the most shocking misinterpretation)? The other assumption is that the present requirements for skill, and education talent, are finite. This is untrue. As far as can be seen, shortages of skill will be a limiting factor in our society for the foreseeable future.

Of course, it doesn't mean, when one says that talented people are not being educated, that people have to be educated like it or not. An awful lot of cant is talked about this. However, it really is pleasanter, in general, to go to university rather than to work in a factory. And, unrepentantly, I do believe that books, pictures and other things associated with 'education' are better than admass.

But even if there is the chance of a meritocracy occurring, there are two fundamental points about the organization of society which it would be well to remember. One is that physical beauty, sex-appeal, creativity, low cunning and so on are *not* measured by any intelligence test but are obviously influential in social life. The same is true of family ties and friendship, which will always help a child whether he is bright or not. The other is that the clever *are* better at doing things. I would rather be operated on by a skilled surgeon than a nice one; and intelligent people do use their knowledge so that life is able to continue and to improve for others.

Would a meritocracy, in any case, be such a disaster? It seems to me that it would at least have the value of being built on the assumption that knowledge and skill are important. This is an advance over the cult of the stupid, which is still a dominant in this country.

At present the danger is not so much that a society stratified by ability will emerge, as that our present inegalitarian trends, which militate against the need of the society for a greater number of people endowed with a higher level of competence than we have at present, will be perpetuated.

In practice concern for equality at the present moment would entail a substantial increase in the public provision of education for children of lesser ability from the working class, both because (compared with children from the middle class and children with higher ability) they are at present housed in worse buildings, frequently taught in larger classes by less enthusiastic teachers, and given fewer playing fields and fewer extra-curricular activities, and also because the handicaps with which they start school life are much greater.

They come from homes where parental concern with their achievement is not high and where frequently the most important factor for developing intelligence – the use of accurate English with a large vocabulary – is uncommon, and from delinquent or semi-delinquent streets. Even if only to prevent delinquency, therefore, the schools must try to overcome these handicaps. The effort would lead to a substantial improvement in the achievements in school of the children from the working class. This in turn would undoubtedly be the quickest and the most effective way of eliminating the social problems of the so-called delinquent areas, a name which masks a much wider social problem – the failure to integrate the unskilled and semi-skilled working class into a society which is becoming predominantly governed by the values and standards of the professional middle class.

It is in this light that one must see the present social role of the schools. It is for this reason that the whole idea of social equality rests upon a substantial increase in educational provision, with a great part of this increase directed towards the kind of children who at present go into the lower streams of the secondary modern schools. Economic policy also points in the same direction. The general failure of our society to provide itself with competent and skilled people is particularly marked at the level of the skilled and semi-skilled workers, and this argument reinforces the argument for greater equality of treatment of children of all abilities and aptitudes.

With a clearer picture in our minds of whom we must now educate and why, let us look at the next stage, at the society for which we are educating them.

CHAPTER THREE

SOCIETY AND THE ECONOMY

IT is worth spending money on education because it assists the economy.

Why? Mainly because it provides a skilled and resilient body of workers at all levels, who help to keep a highly fluid economy going. This is difficult to prove in any precise manner (any proposition in economics is difficult to prove, as a matter of fact). It seems, however, that our economy has been falling behind for many years. The reasons for this are in dispute, but among them the shortage of skilled and educated people certainly stands high. In many respects the United Kingdom has fallen behind its Continental neighbours, not only in its rate of growth, but also in its inventiveness and capacity for change. Although our exports have risen, they have risen less than those of Western Germany or Japan. Our capital assistance to the underdeveloped countries has been on a smaller scale than that of France or the United States, and we have grave difficulty in meeting our international military commitments.

In part this economic weakness arises from our reliance for too long on older basic industries like coal and textiles, which are less appropriate to the world economy than they were fifty or sixty years ago. In part the weakness springs from the lower rate of investment in capital equipment as compared with other countries; but it is now agreed that in recent years the British economy has failed in two things directly related to the education system.

The first is an acute shortage of skilled technicians at all levels which has handicapped the growth of new industries and has been responsible for a failure in design, so that our cars are less efficient and less attractive than those of the

French, our furniture and houses less desirable than those of Scandinavia, our industrial products less up to date than those of Italy.

The second failure has been on the part of the Government and the Civil Service and industry. It is a failure to adapt themselves rapidly to new situations, a general failure of social inventiveness, so that what was heralded as the new Elizabethan age has become a morbid self-interest in backwardness and insularity – a situation brilliantly summarized in Michael Young's pamphlet *The Chipped White Cups of Dover*.

Our cities seem more squalid and dirty than those of our neighbours; we were handicapped until recently by what seemed to be an inability to make elementary decisions over the metric system or to build a Channel tunnel. Whereas our Victorian ancestors built hundreds of miles of railway in a decade, we have not yet constructed more than a few hundred miles of motorway. In almost every field it seems that British resilience and ingenuity have fallen behind. Consequently, it has become necessary for Britain, if she is to become a competitive exporter and eventually an active member of the Common Market, and to play her role in developing the poorer countries of the world, not only to make a substantial leap forward in the knowledge and use of science and technology among all classes and all ability groups, but also to bring forward new and more open-minded people at all levels in business, in government, in the trade unions and in the voluntary societies, so that our country can respond positively to change.

The schools which bear the greatest prestige in our system, and to a certain extent the universities, have been concerned in the past with developing certain traditions of leadership which, while extremely worthy in themselves, lack the positive enthusiasm for ideas and new ways of doing things which is really the hallmark of the best parts of contemporary life, whether in the arts, popular culture or business. These traditions were in a large part a response to nineteenth-century society, when England had a vast overseas empire, when the balance of world economics was in her favour, and when personal independence and initiative were highly prized. This has now become outmoded by the realities of twentieth-century economics, where detailed knowledge, research, technical flair and a clear recognition of the toughness of international competition are of greater value.

Nowhere perhaps is this more necessary than in the City of London and in the top ranks of the Civil Service. It is now universally agreed that the failure of economic policy to control the rise in prices and wages or to allow the economy to grow at its maximum rate mirrors the intellectual failure of the bankers and members of the Civil Service to appreciate the complex nature of the economic problems they have to deal with.

It is the seriousness of this social and intellectual crisis which makes the rapid re-adaptation of our educational system an essential basis for developing the economy.

But it will not be only the leaders who change. The new economy will require a skilled and, because jobs will naturally change so rapidly, a flexible labour force. Many of us will have to be more resilient; many of us will need far more basic skills than we have had in the past in languages, mathematics, and science. It would hardly be an exaggeration to say 'all', for the content of most jobs is almost certain to become increasingly complex. The growth of the economy will also make considerable demands on people, requiring them to learn techniques anew repeatedly during their working lives; and it is quite clear that these techniques will be based more on science and engineering than on any other groups of subjects.

'Manpower forecasting' is a new and somewhat impressionistic skill. It consists of forecasting the requirements for different types of skill in different industries, trades and services for as far ahead as possible. The French, Swedes, Dutch and Americans have done it for a long time, and many countries, including the U.K., have done it for engineers and scientists for a decade or more. It is now gradually being built into British long-term economic forecasting, and both the National Economic Development Council and the Department of Economic Affairs have published estimates which indicate widespread skill shortages. In the nature of things these judgements are largely intuitive – for one thing they cannot really make allowance for technical changes which have not yet occurred – but they have been found in other countries to be a fairly good guide to the direction things are moving in. The general conclusion stands; more skills will be needed; most skills will be more complex; and they will change fairly rapidly.

It follows, therefore, that basic education will need to be more thorough and more general. The economy does not need more apprentices to a particular trade; it needs more people who are sufficiently highly educated to learn quite complicated new methods some years later. Moreover, many of these people will be women coming into the labour force effectively at about the age of thirty or thirty-five, after ten years of being full-time wives and mothers, who will need to compete with men on equal terms.

It is doubtful, too, whether there is any sense in having a rigid division of the academic system by 'ability' (as measured by IQ), because the needs of the economy will be for a range of skills drawn from people of all degrees of ability, rather than for two or three clearly demarcated classes – officers, N.C.O.s, and other ranks. Many people will have overlapping functions, and there will be more team-work than in the past, to replace the boss–foreman–labourer structure of the jobs. All this points to a less rigid division of the secondary schools than exists in most places at the moment. In the long run, England, like other countries, will be driven towards a general education for all up to sixteen, with serious specialization beginning then, according to the individual's ability and vocational interest, as well as his general education's needs.

The Industrial Training Act was passed in 1963 to allow the Government, through the Industrial Training Council, to set up boards covering the greater part of the economy which would assume responsibility for training at all levels. These boards are now coming into operation. They are composed of employers and trades unionists, with people drawn from education as well, and they are financed by a compulsory levy on the firms in their industry. The yield of these levies runs into many millions of pounds. They will provide a stimulus – probably the biggest stimulus for two-thirds of a century – to proper kinds of training.

So we can foresee a change in the economy which will be towards more and more highly qualified people who will frequently have to change their skills and their jobs. Moreover, as the economy changes, so society will change with it. It will become more productive, and the growth of real income may accelerate so that we are within striking distance of a society which could offer middle-class standards of living to all. At the same time, this greater fluidity in the structure of the economy will be accompanied by the decline of staple industries like coal and agriculture and the rise of the service trades will be accompanied by a movement – more rapid than we have ever known before – towards the sort of middle-class life that has become characteristic of the more prosperous suburbs.

It has become customary to attack this tendency as a growth of materialism, increasing, as it does, people's pre-occupation with material possessions of all kinds. In fact, what is perhaps most noticeable even today is the great growth in the participation of ordinary people in non-material pursuits of all kinds. Every index which is known of active participation in sport, art, or amateur dramatics has risen, and there has probably never been a generation in England which has so avidly read serious books, listened to serious music, or been as politically mature or concerned as the present one.

Perhaps the most profound social change which this altered economy has already brought about is in the structure of the family. The age of marriage has fallen; the number of people getting married has risen. Within marriage the unequal roles of man and wife have been replaced by something like a partnership. Women in America now go back to work at thirty, as their families are at school; here it is nearer thirty-five – but they have in any case over a quarter of a century of active working life outside the home after they have become to some extent free of their families.

While the family unit has been changing, family life has also become more important. This is sometimes regarded as a sign of the English people's desire to look in on themselves, to become increasingly self-sufficient and less open to new ideas and to change. This would, I think, be a mistaken interpretation. There is a great deal of evidence that the relationships of men and women in our society, and the treatment of children, are less neurotic and less prone to emotional instability than in earlier ages. At the same time, the enthusiasm of young people for travelling, for welcoming change, and for striking out on their own must be a sign of a new degree of mental health and security in the typical family.

But not all our recent social change has been for the better. There are two major exceptions. The first is the apparent spread of delinquency and social breakdown among young people in areas where primary poverty (to which delinquency was often previously attributed) no longer prevails. The second is the growth of an autonomous adolescent culture which is in part often blamed for the increasing tendency of young people – or the apparently increasing tendency of young people – to break the law. In fact the growth of delinquency has been overestimated, and will continue to be overestimated both by the tendentious way the statistics are presented and also by the extraordinary preoccupation of some newspapers with petty misdemeanours. But it is true that crimes of violence, theft, dangerous driving, and other irresponsible, anti-social activities prevail, whether or not they have actually increased in volume relatively to the population at risk.

The schools have been held to blame for this. But if they are indeed to blame, it is neither because of their lax discipline nor because of the use of modern methods. The cause can only be that their curricula and teaching methods have not been fully adapted to the needs and interests of a potentially delinquent population; and above all, that the areas where delinquency is common often have schools which are the least well served in terms of buildings and staff. Here social policy would surely dictate an immense increase in the number of highly qualified staff and a substantial provision of playing-fields and out-of-school activities, to compensate for the lack of elementary social provision in the area.

But the blame cannot, of course, simply be laid on the schools. The problem is a much wider one – it is that of a new generation said to be autonomous and independent of the values of its parents and of its teachers; its allegiance is owed primarily to other members of that generation rather than to the values of society at large. Inevitably in a society where values have changed as rapidly as they have in our own there will be a gap between people of different ages and between their frames of reference which arise directly from contrasting experiences.

What can be agreed is that young people are now more self-reliant, that they are more scientifically minded, that they are less prone than earlier generations to take on trust what their elders tell them. But this is simply a further step towards the extension of pragmatic scientific principles into ordinary life – which most of us accept in theory (although not so often in practice) – while it is at the same time a recognition by young people of the value of self-respect and of respect for human individuality, both of which have long been preached and accepted in public in the adult world.

Thus the economy and the society are changing, and must continue to change. But to service this economy and society – a 'middle-class' society – we need a different sort of education. We need, above all, more teachers, better teachers, a different kind of teacher. Where are we to get them?

CHAPTER FOUR

NEW ATTITUDES AND
NEW TECHNIQUES

TO staff our schools adequately in the 1970s we need at least 100,000 more teachers. We shall not find them quickly. We must therefore think of new ways of teaching.

One of the most discouraging results of the contemplative study of education has been to distract attention from the changes that take place in how it is done. In fact changes have often taken place, even in the teaching of traditional subjects like Latin. They take place not only, for example, when people come to understand more about the structure of Latin, or about the way children understand and perceive a language, or about the emotional difficulties inherent in the teaching relationship – all of which are quite fundamental; but also in such simple matters as the redesigning of textbooks, and in the use of pictures, charts, and diagrams, or of plays and films. With a subject like French, which is alive in the sense that Latin is not, the use of television, tape-recorders, visits to France, and so on are more and more replacing the formal construing of sentences.

In the teaching of Russian, conventional methods just cannot be used, as there is an absolute shortage of teachers of Russian. In the whole U.S.A. in 1960, twenty-three new teachers of Russian were qualified. Television, tape-recorders, and 'immersion courses' are essential if more than a handful of people are to learn Russian – and who can doubt that hundreds of thousands of us should? For scientists, especially, it is far more important than German or French.

Mathematics has also been revolutionized. We now realize that it is a language, and can therefore be taught as a system of communication. We know that notions of quantity, weight, distance – all mathematical relationships – are matters of total perception and that a whole wealth of teaching aids has to be called into play if mathematics is to be understood by the child who has no natural gift for numbers.

These questions about particular subjects raise a more basic issue. How far is it possible to do a more effective job in education, using existing resources, by reallocating them and using them in new ways, with new aids?

Take some extreme examples. In the University of London, Birkbeck College is largely unused during the day because it is a college for people who also hold full-time jobs; a great many rooms elsewhere are hardly used after 5 p.m. Much of the University, apart from the research laboratories and libraries, and the administrative offices, is almost empty for four months of the year. Why should undergraduates be free from mid-June to mid-October? Why should the school day for some teachers last from 9 a.m. to 4 p.m.? And why should they have twelve weeks' holiday a year? The under-utilization of plant and staff is remarkable.

There are, of course, good reasons for these practices. It is often impractical to use rooms twice – once for day students and once for evening students – if equipment has to be left out, books kept on shelves, and notes in desks – just as it would be impractical to produce ballet at Covent Garden in the morning, opera in the afternoon, and intimate revue in the late evening. Teachers become emotionally exhausted, and they must have time to read, to write, to travel, and to attend courses.

Children need rest from severe intellectual effort. But it may be that some children learn more, and are happier, with only four weeks' holiday a year. In other cases, by re-arranging our system people could actually learn more in a shorter period, if they worked harder. It is also the case that if they worked more days in the year, the intensity of much of the school day could be reduced (as I explain below); and certainly one of the easiest ways to raise teachers' pay is to ask them to work more. It is by no means self-evident, as teachers claim, that teaching is more exhausting emotionally and intellectually than – say – being a surgeon, a psychiatrist, or a newspaper reporter, whose holidays are far shorter.

I have raised these questions because they are the sort of questions naturally asked about other areas of the economy. Why should they not be asked also of education? As productivity rises in other parts of the economy, it has often been said that in education and in the other service trades it has not risen proportionately. Consequently, by comparison with other goods, education has become more expensive. In other words, any extension of the education system is thought by economists to be more expensive now than it was some years ago, and this is reflected in the fact that teachers' salaries have tended to rise faster than the average increase in the rest of the economy.

The analysis is not inevitably correct, because those who make it have neglected the fact that techniques in education have changed radically in the course of history under the pressure of new knowledge, and knowledge of teaching techniques has from time to time changed profoundly. There has been a revolution in our knowledge of the psychology of the learning process, and in the knowledge of child psychology and many problems of adolescence, a revolution as important as that produced by many medical discoveries.

In another way, too, productivity in education has risen. Printers and publishers have learnt how to produce books for the schools which are easier to read, and the material is presented more effectively and in the correct sequence for easier assimilation. The most simple proof of this is to compare the primers used in teaching reading fifty years ago with those in use in infant schools today, or to compare a manual for teaching French published in the late 1880s with those at present in use. On visual grounds alone they are easier to comprehend, and this represents a revolution in typography, in paper-making, and in the order in which the material is presented. It is now far easier to learn to read, or to learn to read French, than it was half a century ago.

But even those who admit that techniques in education change often believe that they change less rapidly than techniques in industry. This makes them think that education, together with other service trades, represents a stagnant part of the economy which in some senses 'lives off the fat' of the more rapidly developing parts. Because many people share these beliefs, the contribution of education to the economy has always been underestimated, for there has been no measure by which the statisticians have been able to evaluate it. As a further consequence, teachers have never been encouraged to regard themselves, like other workers, as people with the duty of increasing the effectiveness of what they are trying to do.

This phrase 'increase the effectiveness of their work', of course, has nasty connotations. An attempt to 'increase educational productivity' sounds dangerously like an attempt to mass-produce a well-instructed but fundamentally ill-educated nation. But it still remains the case that even theology can be effectively or ineffectively taught; and by 'increasing productivity' all that is meant is reducing the amount of effort by teachers and taught in acquiring a given amount of knowledge, or in acquiring an attitude, or in improving their physiques, or whatever the aim may be at any particular time. No judgement is passed as to the ends, merely as to the means of achieving them.

Even on the most material grounds, teachers would do well to look to their productivity. It has been observed by Sir Geoffrey Crowther that if this attitude towards their job were more consciously adopted by educators, as it has been over the broad field of industry, the result would be to improve the bargaining position of teachers; because by working more effectively they would provide themselves with arguments for raising their salaries exactly analogous to those of industrial workers who by raising their productivity justify wage awards.

But in all this there is a point of greater educational significance. Much of the education system at the moment is ineffective. Everyone admits this. One suspects that the reason why it is ineffective – and why remedies for its improvement seem to be unacceptable – is that the idea of trying to work out how productive a given educational process actually is remains a strange one to most individuals and most authorities. Consequently, when decisions are taken which are in essence decisions about the use of resources, they get lost beneath a series of arguments about philosophy and doctrine. Let us take two examples: the arguments about the comprehensive school and about modern methods of teaching. In both cases one of the essential arguments for adopting the policy at issue is that the teaching is more effective; that children of all abilities learn more, and retain more effectively what they have learnt or have been taught, in a comprehensive school under conditions of free discipline. Another is that children taught in a comprehensive school, or under free conditions, become more mature and more relaxed in later life. These are statements of a positive nature which can be tested by observation and experiment. But observation and experiment are simply not applied. As a result, the whole argument has been couched in terms of 'the position of the *élite*', or the 'need for discipline'. To my mind this attempt to philosophize about questions which are largely matters of fact represents a significant retreat from rational methods of discourse.

In the remainder of this chapter I want to take two instances of the way new knowledge and new techniques could change and are changing education. The first is the effect of child psychology on the primary schools, where teaching techniques have developed rapidly in the last thirty years, but where organization lags behind. The second is the teaching of mathematics in a highly technological society.

The primary schools are one of the good things in English education. The children are happy, the teachers are relaxed and efficient, and some of the new buildings are very beautiful.

They are chronically short of teachers, of course. Partly, one supposes, because they have never been thought important; partly because they rely on women teachers, and the changing pattern of marriage has taken many of them out of the schools. Obviously, then, the primary school's ultimate salvation lies in the training of more teachers. Their success, too, emphasizes the importance of teacher-training; the teachers are good because they have been taught how to teach: because they understand child psychology and the problems of teaching basic skills like reading and writing. The schools are happy because the teachers are competent.

However, the time is ripe for a change of attitude to the primary schools, which are still *organized* as they were fifty years ago. We are the only country in the world to impose a five-year-old entry age, for a five-hour day, which in many ways is too long; it is wasteful of teachers' time and it is sometimes positively upsetting to the children. On the other hand, there is a demand for far more nursery schools for the under-fives. Nursery classes have been proved, over and over again, to be not only convenient for the working mothers of young children, of whom there will probably always be some – deserted, unmarried, widowed, bored, or just poor – but also immensely helpful to the mental health and growth of ordinary children, who get bored at home and want company in a calm atmosphere free from strain, which only a trained teacher can engender. They are also an excellent preparation for full-time schooling.

I would favour making school part-time to the age of six, and opening up more afternoon nursery classes to make use of the teachers' time; or alternatively running two sessions a day with classes half their present size. In terms of sheer effectiveness of teaching, there can be little doubt that the children would get on better, and in terms of their happiness, a shorter day would have much to recommend it.

At the other end of the primary school there are several possible changes which could be made. The gradual elimination of the 11 plus, by reducing or eliminating selection at eleven, is reducing much of the cramming and excessive streaming which is the bane of so many of the top classes of the junior schools at the moment.

In place of the cramming, there is much to be said for introducing elementary science and the beginnings of a foreign language, at least for the more able children. The strength of the private prep-schools has been that they have made the children work harder at a greater number of academic subjects; and a number of recent experiments in the primary schools suggest that children of average ability and above enjoy learning French at an early age, while science can be taught to all groups.

The recent investigations of primary schools by the Plowden Committee have confirmed most strikingly the analysis just presented. There is no doubt that 'modern methods' of freedom and experiment in the classroom are much more successful – in every sense of the word – than old-fashioned methods. There is no doubt, too, that we are on the verge of a big period of further experiment in what to teach and how to teach.

One major issue is the age at which the children should transfer from the primary school to a secondary school. At present it is at 11; in the private sector, however, it is at 13. The consensus of opinion seems to be that 12 is the right age; and if this is so, then the pattern of primary education might be an (optional) nursery school from 3 to 6; a first school from 6 to 9; and a junior school from 9 to 12.

In addition, during the period of grave teacher shortage, it seems likely that the teachers in primary schools have been wise to accept assistants to do the many things that require little or no specific pedagogic skill. Occasionally, the teachers have resisted this, as it has seemed that they would be opening the way to a dilution of the teaching profession. Either the untrained assistants would take over part of the teachers' proper job, it was feared, or they would be given a short period of training which would be a quick back door into teaching. Many people think that these fears are unjustified; doctors have nurses to help them without a constant fear that the nurses will suddenly start taking out people's appendixes, and though the analogy of teaching with medicine is a little forced, it has some degree of validity. That teachers in practice welcome assistants seems obvious, however.

And they will also start to use far more of the new techniques – machines, television and radio – to supplement their own work. But it is not only in the primary schools that the shortage of teachers and changing technology makes the adoption of new techniques both vital and possible. In our technological and scientific culture, mathematics is an essential mode of thought. Above all, we need a revolution in the teaching of mathematics at all levels. The innumeracy with which we are cursed as a nation starts in the primary school and continues throughout the whole system.

It has often been demonstrated that only those who are extremely fortunate in their mathematics teachers, or those who, whether by nature or by some quirk of environment, appear to have mathematical minds, really grasp mathematics in the present state of mathematics teaching in Britain. Even at this deplorable standard we have far too few teachers and over the next ten to fifteen years the shortage is likely to get worse. Short courses provided by local authorities and the extra effort of the training colleges are drops in the ocean. The situation is almost hopeless.

But it has been shown in a number of experiments in Europe and America that a great deal of what is at present taught in schools is irrelevant and out-of-date, and furthermore, that by using up-to-date text books – well designed and well presented – by using models, by using the new techniques of teaching which psychologists who have studied the learning process have developed, schools can teach ordinary children, who have appeared up to now to be unresponsive, to develop their mathematical knowledge and their fundamental mathematical insight rapidly. Since the primary schools have been the seat of English experimental education for many years, and it is their techniques which have spread upwards into the secondary schools (and from them into higher education), it would seem extremely important to try to pour all the effort possible into raising the standards of primary-school mathematics teaching. In essence this means encouraging the teachers to use the new techniques which are being developed in the United States. In America, brilliant young mathematicians, psychologists, and teachers have sat down together and developed new courses in mathematics, and it is quite clear that if administrative drive can be put behind effort of this sort the primary teachers in this country will be enthusiastic in taking them up, for the primary schools have always been the most willing to experiment with new ideas in the past.

The Department of Education and Science both directly and through the Schools Council has begun to initiate far-reaching research and innovation in this field, and so has the Nuffield Foundation. It has been found that the university teachers of mathematics – and of science – are eager to take part in this work. In 1960 it looked as though nothing would ever happen, but already the speed of change is remarkable.

But a fundamental reappraisal of the whole structure and

technique of education from primary schools to university level is essential, and the time has come for the technological achievements of our civilization to be brought into the educational system in full force. This means, first, a rational analysis of the job to be done. An enormous amount of present-day learning in the schools could on rational examination be found to be quite purposeless, whilst a substantial amount of what would be useful is not taught; and what is taught, whether purposeful or purposeless, is often being taught extremely inefficiently. By careful study of the learning process, and of the order in which children acquire knowledge of a new subject – which is, after all, the essence of teaching – a substantial improvement could be made. This has been shown in teaching skills to new entrants to industry. Time and time again it has been shown that people who lack ability can be taught relatively complicated new methods of doing a job in quite a short time, and taught very effectively, provided that the teaching has been programmed and is designed to fit their needs. Similar skills are inefficiently taught over a great deal of time by the hit-and-miss method of apprenticeship.

It means, secondly, a desire to experiment radically. Experiments here and in America have shown that the classroom itself is becoming an out-of-date concept. In a school in Massachusetts, I have seen a group of children being taught by a team of teachers – one teacher reading a story to a small group, another working with individual children who had been away because of illness, yet another preparing the next lesson, and some children studying by themselves under the supervision of an adult. By the use of this 'team-teaching' technique, teachers of varying ability and varying degrees of professional competence can be used appropriately, and newly trained teachers, or teachers in training, can easily be fitted into the team and given jobs suited to their level of skill and confidence. If to this sort of team-teaching approach

– which is now accepted in a number of schools – is added the free use of machines, tape-recorders, television, and other devices, we may look forward to a time when the conventional streaming or setting of schools, or even the division of schools between primary and secondary levels, are seen to impose rigidities on the learning process which are unnecessary and harmful.

Some may say at this point that the whole emphasis on effective techniques is anti-educational in tone, but this is a view I find difficult to understand. One of the major purposes of education, although obviously not the only one, is that children should learn what they are taught. It is known that in the existing situation a great many do not. It is moreover recognized that this failure to learn is itself responsible for and in part springs from a deep maladjustment in the individual child, which manifests itself later (or at that time) in personality difficulties and delinquency. I suspect that at the bottom of the argument lies the feeling that the more equipment comes between the child and the teacher the less the teacher is able to have a personal influence on the child. It is felt that the influence of the teacher – an influence which he wields because he is a mature person – is much more important than, say, whether he can actually teach the child to analyse the elements of a chemical compound.

This, it seems, to me, is based upon a misconception. A teacher who is effective in teaching what he sets out to teach will be more highly regarded by his pupils than one who has not succeeded; and if a teacher can be relieved of the mechanical tasks which at present compose a great deal of his professional life, he will find it easier to be relaxed with his pupils.

Let us, for example, take the head teacher preparing a time-table. For many heads this involves days of pacing about putting complex diagrams on pieces of paper spread over the floor, and a feeling of constant anxiety lest three classes should meet in one classroom while two teachers are left completely unoccupied for a whole morning. This sort of problem could be solved in five minutes by an electronic computer and it is amazing that for so long education authorities were unwilling to experiment in this field. Now they are beginning to do so and are finding that not only are the timetables more effectively designed – for you can give computers such statements as 'Miss Smith must never teach in the next room to Mr Jones because his voice is too loud', whereas even the best head-teacher cannot remember more than about twenty such facts – but also head-teachers are relieved of a great deal of unproductive labour, leaving them free to get to know their children. A trivial example, perhaps, but it shows the extent to which technical obsolescence in education has been preventing the teachers from concentrating on their proper and serious task.

In this chapter I have discussed the many changes that are taking place in what is taught and the way it is taught. In the next I shall examine some of the consequences of the new education in the secondary schools – which are in many ways the strategic centre of our education system.

CHAPTER FIVE

DIFFERENTIATION AND SELECTION

In England we have always, until very recently, had different types of schools for different types of children. There they were intended to learn different groups of subjects, because it was thought that children came in layers – clever children (seventeen per cent) who were able to study classics, mathematics, foreign languages, science, and other 'difficult' subjects at grammar schools; not-so-clever children who were to do technical subjects at technical schools (five per cent); and then the great mass, who were to be hewers of wood and drawers of water, able to live life fully, doubtless, but not with the aid of books. Topping it all stood the public, semi-public and private schools – taking about ten per cent of the children and leading to many of the best jobs. Entry was almost entirely by purchase tempered by ability. Winchester takes the top one per cent of the top five per cent or ten per cent of income receivers, as a recent American writer has put it.

These independent schools have flourished and grown as the number of people able to afford them has increased. Their record has improved; they are far less reactionary and stupid than they were; some are good schools. But it is ridiculous that some of the best schools should be available only to the rich. This is today so obvious that it is unnecessary to argue the case any more. Ever since the Fleming Report (1945) argued for the eventual full entry of pupils from the maintained schools into the public schools, the discussion has not been about ends but about means. How can such an incorporation of the private sector into the public sector be achieved without either ending the right of parents to buy education for their children, or creaming off the cleverest and nicest-speaking boys and girls from the maintained primary schools? One answer given by the Public Schools Commission was to draw up plans for each school, keeping its individual character, and that a large number of working-class children should be encouraged to apply for admission. There is some evidence that there are many ordinary working-class families who would like their children to board for a year or two, or even longer. But how high a priority should be given to this preference? And will schools of this kind be desirable?

Apart from selection by wealth, the realization that dividing children up according to 'types' not only shows a misguided attitude towards the children, a mistaken idea of their differing abilities, but is quite inappropriate to our modern economic needs, has gradually dawned on the country.

Consequently, the biggest changes in education since the war have taken place in the secondary schools. The grammar schools were made free schools entirely for children of high ability, whereas previously they combined clever scholarship winners with children of lesser ability from the lower middle classes whose parents could afford the subsidized fees. Before the war most of their sixth forms were very small; and as recently as 1954 the authorities were worried by the high proportion of children who left school at fifteen. In recent years, however, the number of children who have left before taking O level has become negligible, and the rate of growth of sixth forms is about five per cent a year. Very soon these grammar schools – which provide one-fifth of the places available under government secondary education for children at eleven – will be schools affording a complete education to all their entrants from the age of eleven (or whatever the age of transfer is) to the age of eighteen or nineteen.

Apart from a small number of secondary technical schools, most children over eleven receive their education in secondary modern schools. These are the descendants of the old senior elementary schools. They too have suffered – or enjoyed – a series of profound changes since 1947, when the school-leaving age was raised to fifteen, thus increasing the length of the course they gave by one-third. Since then the greater part of secondary-school building has been concentrated on new secondary modern schools. The formal qualifications of their teachers have risen dramatically, and in the last few years the number of children staying on beyond the school-leaving age of sixteen or even to eighteen and taking external examinations has grown substantially. Small all-age schools have nearly all disappeared and, despite the existence of far too many dreary ex-elementary school buildings, within this decade it is possible to hope that almost all secondary modern schools will be much better (both physically and in terms of the qualifications of their teachers) than was ever thought possible fifteen years ago.

Nevertheless, there is still a great deal of hostility to the secondary modern school, and it is virtually impossible to find any middle-class child in them; allocation to a secondary modern school is almost universally regarded as a 'failure' in the 11 plus. Despite the fact that selection at eleven is supposed to be by objective tests of ability and attainment, the grammar schools still consist to a high degree of middle-class children, to the exclusion of children of the manual and semi-skilled working classes. Because of this, the reputation of the secondary modern schools has lagged far behind that of grammar schools.

However, in areas where the secondary modern schools have become well established it is said that tension in the 11 plus is less acute than it once was.

Indeed, it is sometimes said that the arguments over the reorganization of secondary education were really over the problems arising from the transition period. When the new schools had been built and fifth- and sixth-year courses introduced into all schools, the differing status of grammar and modern would die down. We should be on the threshold of 'secondary education for all'.

But is this really true? Are we not right to try to speed up the process of change, and was not this 'gradualist' approach inappropriate to our near-crisis conditions?

The debate about the meaning of the phrase 'secondary education for all' has raged for twenty years. It seems a travesty of the aim of giving equal treatment to all children, to send some at the age of eleven to a well-equipped, well-staffed, old-established school, while others (in effect) stay on at their old elementary schools. Would it not still seem a travesty if there remained a division between schools not just in equipment but in status?

TWO DEBATES

The debate tends to confuse two issues. One is about the type of school; the other is about selection.

In 1945 and 1946, when post-war restrictions meant that there were few teachers and no new buildings, it was obviously unfair that less than a fifth of the child population at the age of eleven should have very much more spent on them than the rest. But if it could be shown that they were of a different nature from the remaining four-fifths, then the public might accept it. The two defences for this policy were not really very good, although many people were taken in for a while. First, it was argued that you could easily tell a 'grammar-school child' from the rest, and that his needs were very different from those of the average child. But it was extremely difficult to choose the cleverest children without obvious unfairness at the margin; of every hundred children, of whom twenty went to a grammar school, seven who were not chosen might have got in if the examination had been held on a different day, and seven who did make the grade might not. So the choice was extremely bad, and in the nature of the case was bound to be so, because ability is a continuum, with no sharp division between the two groups of the able and the less able. But the second defence, that ability cannot be acquired, was also bad, because not all sorts of education are related to ability; and 'ability' is not an objective characteristic – it covers motivation and background to an exceptional degree. So that, for example, the grammar school has never aimed exclusively at training the super-intelligent; in its emphasis on sport, and on 'character', and on good manners and civilized behaviour, it has shared in a tradition that is to an important degree independent of ability.

When it could be shown, too, that being chosen for a grammar school – and even more, success in it – was based to an important extent upon parental background (which for short was called 'social class'), it seemed even more patently unfair that these fortunate and able children should have an education based on good teachers and playing fields, while their neighbours from poor homes were denied all this. At first sight, indeed, it might seem that if there was a shortage of good schools and good teachers they should be used to redress the balance of the less-favoured homes; that the more fortunate could much better fend for themselves.

The grammar schools, of course, could claim – and rightly – that their main duty was to pass on an academic heritage; the country needed educated and skilled people, and (in the given circumstances) they had to do what they could with the material on hand. Nevertheless, for the most part they failed – and often disastrously – with one group of their pupils, who, being unable to accept academic or social discipline, left early in a state of antagonism to their school. While it is true that a large number of working-class boys and girls were happy and successful at grammar schools – and this is no new phenomenon, it is sixty years old – the great majority of 'early leavers' were from the working-class.

All this makes it seem clear that schools will in future have to be less selective – they will offer a wider range of courses to a wider range of children. Whether there will be big 'comprehensive' schools as in London, or schools with a break at fourteen as in Leicestershire, seems a matter of detail. Above all, the public schools must be 'brought into' the system somehow.

Let us now look at the two complex questions of selection and whether or not to have separate kinds of school at all.

SELECTION

Any breaking down of barriers between secondary and grammar schools will make selection arrangements far easier because they will be less irrevocable. Before 1944 there were two alternative bases of selection – parental income, or outstanding talent; since 1944 segregation has been based largely on ability on a particular day in early spring. The argument against this segregation is strengthened by the virtual absence of arrangements for the transfer of late developers, and the high probability that such arrangements will fail because a 'late transfer' is inadequately prepared for his new school, for example having little or no background in languages, mathematics, or science. And this absence of transfer makes the decision at eleven (an age which stands condemned on psychological grounds also) a decision barring the great majority from taking the examinations which are essential for entry to the better-paid jobs, the professions, and the universities. In other words, this admittedly imperfect selection on educational grounds has permanent effects in closing the doors of opportunity to an enormous number of children.

But it still remains true that there are clever children and backward children, even though it is far harder to tell them apart at eleven than psychologists used to think. Surely they do have different needs?

The question of measuring intelligence is complicated, and has almost passed beyond the comprehension of the layman.

Nevertheless, the issues involved affect us all, and, having reviewed the evidence to the best of their ability, laymen must decide what course of action is best.

Intelligence is made up of a number of factors, some of them inherent and others acquired by learning from the very moment of birth. The differences brought about by environment are considerable, and greatly affect the differences in measured ability which appear between children of different social classes. It used to be thought that these differences were a reflection of the larger families born to less able people, but it seems that a majority of psychologists would now hold that what these differences really reveal are the cumulative effects of cultural impoverishment on the one hand, and the increasing effects of a high standard of civilization on the other. By manipulating the environment a great deal of apparent stupidity could be eliminated.

Nevertheless, differences would still remain even if all children from their earliest months were given the sort of advantages which now accrue to the children of parents in the professional classes. The question is, are the differences which would remain so great that to all intents and purposes the children are basically so far apart that they need different sorts of schooling? Here the evidence is far less clear. It is certain that cultural differences will remain important for a great many years to come. It will therefore be extremely difficult to educate the backward children from extremely poor homes together with the clever children from professional homes. It will be difficult on two grounds – the problem of teaching them together will be almost insuperable for the average teacher, and most of the parents in the professional groups will not allow it. But even supposing that these difficulties could be overcome, differences between the very clever children and the very stupid children might still be so great that it would be impracticable – and unkind – to educate them together.

The case is not clear-cut. In some countries children of all abilities are taught together until a comparatively late age; in other countries they are divided at six or seven. In Norway, for example, selection and streaming in ordinary schools is illegal. It seems to be agreed that below the age of six the differences are not important, but that above the age of sixteen they clearly are so. At what age, then, between six and sixteen, should the selection be made?

The issue seems to be a mixture of ideology and practicality. If it were left to the teachers, some division would take place because of the problems inherent in trying to teach together children with a wide range of ability. Many grammar-school teachers place great value and emphasis on hard work and achievement, a view which the children often share, but this type of tradition depends on working with able and cooperative children.

As long as separate provision for different groups of the community exists, there is bound to be a problem of selection. At primary-school level this is largely done by geographical zoning. For independent schools it is done by the purse, tempered by birth and brains. For grammar schools it is done by IQ, and for universities by attainment, tempered by the lottery of 'knowing the ropes'. All these systems are unfair. It is a matter of doubt which of them is the least pernicious. But as selection at one level or another is bound to last for many years, the important thing is that it should be done well.

But there is a basic dilemma in all selection procedures. Selection by attainment is one of the best predictors of success, and at university level seems obviously fair, so that a boy with good A levels is preferred to one with poor A levels; but all the same (and this is recognized at the 11 plus) a boy from a big and famous school is likely to have been much better taught than a boy from a small unknown school, so that the better-taught boy – if 'fairness' means anything –

should be handicapped. The dilemma is, of course, that the boy from the bigger school *by this test* is better able to get down to his degree work; and if the country needs more first-class honours men more quickly, it should take the 'better' boy because his chance of getting a first is higher.

But the country's needs are less specific than this. It needs more trained talent, but it can do with it over a broader range than a few firsts; and above all it needs a far wider spread of education. This entails a wider spread of opportunity; but tests of attainment for entry tend to raise the hurdles against the candidates from the weaker schools and to accentuate the problems of cramming and over-specialization. That is to say, they limit the spread of opportunity by placing the prizes effectively beyond the grasp of the majority of schools. For example, there are many primary schools which rarely send a child to a grammar school, many grammar schools which rarely send a boy to one of the bigger universities, and so on.

The Americans have an even greater dilemma. Our differences are those of social class; the primary schools which 'do badly' tend to be in almost exclusively manual-working-class areas. In America these differences are also of colour. A 'poor' primary school is largely Negro, or Puerto Rican, or Italian. America also has problems connected with the wide diversity of school systems over her whole continent. It is difficult to get nation-wide examinations at more than elementary level – or comparable to our A level – universally accepted as valid.

What they do is interesting to us, because we are now entering a period of broad secondary education leading to a wide range of higher courses for which the problems of selection are gigantic. Broadly speaking, in some American systems, schools are graded into a number of categories – say 'A' to 'E' – in such a way that the top twenty per cent of pupils in 'B' schools are equal to the second twenty per cent of the pupils in the 'A' schools, and so on down the line. Then the tests are scaled for the category of your school. So, to give a simplified example, if you come from grade 'E', where the *top* twenty per cent will be equal to the bottom twenty per cent of the 'A' grades, then you will be given extra marks. In the external examinations, the schools range their pupils in order themselves, placing and choosing the top twenty of 'A' and the top twenty of 'B'; but the adjustments which make sure that 'A' 20 equals 'B' 1 are made externally.

A similar system was used in parts of the West Riding for entry to grammar schools. A quota of West Riding grammar-school places was allocated to each primary school; one which habitually sent four pupils will itself nominate four, and the marginal fourth and fifth boys and girls were interviewed and tested to see that they were at the same standard as marginal boys and girls from other schools (which may send eight or ten pupils a year to the grammar schools). If they were better, the school's quota was raised; if worse, it was reduced. (The tests are of course scaled for age.) Gradually, too, the aim could be to adjust the quotas to bring them to a greater degree of equality.

It seems to me a fundamentally sound principle of selection that each supplying school should be given a quota, which it selects itself, while the adjustments of the quota should be done by a joint committee of the giving and receiving schools and colleges.

The advantages of putting the onus of selection on the sending rather than the receiving school is very great, because it allows schools to experiment with their curricula without tying them to the entrance requirements of any other institution. The disadvantages are obvious; the teachers could be accused of favouritism and so on. But the example I have given is illustrative of the general problem that selection entails: it is both restrictive of freedom, and it allows accusations of unfairness to be brought. That is why selection is always under fire.

SCHOOLS – ONE AND INDIVISIBLE?

Should there be any separate kinds of school at all? It is probable, as I have already shown, that the independent schools will one day be incorporated into the public sector of education. Indeed, a number of theories have been put forward to account for their continued existence outside it; one is the ingrained snobbery of the English, another is the inadequacy of the maintained schools, and a third is the intense and somewhat surprising piety of the English middle class, which demands the Christian virtues of schools originally endowed for the poor. Whatever the reasons for their continuance, the schools themselves say that they wish to end their isolation.

What can be done with these institutions in the modern education system? There are in fact questions to answer at three levels of analysis. The first inquiry can be conducted in what are commonly called 'real' terms. The buildings, the pupils and the teachers exist. If they can all be brought into the publicly owned sector of education, there will be an improvement in the average level of that sector, because the private schools have more favourable pupil–teacher ratios, and on the whole better buildings and playing fields. Thus the pupil from the public school would be taught in larger classes, and the average pupil from the maintained school would be taught in smaller classes. This would apply particularly in science – especially mathematics and physics, where the public schools have taken more than their fair share of the most able mathematics and physics teachers by offering them more favourable conditions and salaries, while the maintained schools have been short of these specialists. Thus at the 'real' level there is no problem in incorporating the private schools into the public system of education.

The second question is how this could be paid for. At present something like £60 million per year is spent on school fees. If all these boys and girls were brought into the maintained system and there were no decline in the level of amenities offered, there would be an increase in public expenditure of this amount. Compared with the total bill for education this is of course small, but in relation to the overall demand of the social services for increased outlays it represents a small but significant increase in the demands on the taxpayer.

Thirdly there is the legal and political problem of how the incorporation would take place. The Labour Government established the Public Schools Commission charged with the task of incorporating the public schools into the maintained system in the most appropriate manner. It was a failure.

It therefore seems necessary to put forward concrete proposals for the incorporation of individual schools into the maintained system. We are not, I think, concerned with the many second- and third-rate private schools which exist, particularly in southern England. Many of these will be closed when the requirements for teaching in private schools are as severe as the requirements for maintained schools. In any case, they represent a different social problem from that of the public schools. Certainly no academic claims that they make can be taken seriously. Most of the public schools, however, represent serious educational enterprises.

For the hundred or so major schools there have been a number of proposals either to turn them into comprehensive boarding schools (because there is a great need for boarding provision for children of average or less than average ability, as recent inquiries have shown), or to turn them into junior colleges of the universities, to cater for pupils of seventeen to nineteen who intend to go on to a full honours degree course, or for those who will terminate their studies by a liberal arts course. All these proposals were rejected.

Some schools, of course, may continue to be for academic 'flyers', others will be for Roman Catholics, or Jews. But the essential principle is that choice should not be restricted by parental income, but should be based upon some objective criterion. In all the schools tuition would be free, but the boarding and maintenance element would be subject to a parental means test. The day schools would be analogous to the present secondary schools. The difficulty is that no objective criterion can be found. The wisest course, it seems to many, is to leave the schools alone.

What about the direct-grant grammar schools? They are good schools, with immensely valuable achievements. There is a strong case for fully incorporating them into the public system. But should grammar schools of any sort survive at all? Their existence requires selection, which we have seen is bound to be inadequate and harmful, and there are strong arguments that the selection at eleven is mainly responsible for the 'streaming by ability' which dominates English schools from the primary schools on, with the consequence that a child initially placed in a low stream will be conditioned to a 'B'-stream mentality. There is much evidence that this is psychologically and socially harmful; and two great countries, Russia and America, manage to run education systems without using streaming.

Yet there is an element of sentimentality in these arguments; whatever may be thought about the nature of ability, by the time a child goes to school differences do exist, and the average English teacher finds it easier to teach a fairly narrow range of ability and background. Nor, I think, is it possible by putting clever and dull children side by side to hide from them that some of them are clever and some dull, even if we know that the words 'clever' and 'dull' often mean 'better off' and 'worse off'. And it is unlikely that the school by itself will redress the balance of a society which tends to reward the successful, forceful, and intelligent.

Some, indeed, would feel that what the country needs is more intelligence, and that there is a case for more not less selection *for teaching purposes*. That is to say, children should be 'setted' for each subject, including physical education and

58

music, and the common background of their lives should be found outside the school. In this view the school is predominantly a place where you learn things; it is noticeable that the main opponents of streaming are teachers (chiefly teachers of English) who teach subjects where, in their opinion, knowledge and skill in a technique are not as important as the proper emotional response. A rugger master, for example, would not welcome the unstreaming of his four XV's.

It is against this background that the comprehensive school has been introduced. Its introduction has been accompanied by a whole series of irrelevancies. One is the great size of the London schools. This is the result of three things which are not necessary conditions for a comprehensive school. First, it is a London tradition to have big schools; the original London School Board schools in the 1870s were for a roll of 1,500 to 2,000 children. Secondly, it was based on the arithmetical calculation in 1937 that only five per cent of the children would stay on to the sixth forms, for whom an adequate variety of specialist teachers had to be provided. It is extremely probable that the percentage will ultimately be at least thirty per cent. In these circumstances a comprehensive school of 900 would be economic. Thirdly, land in London is scarce and expensive, and big schools take less space than several small ones.

Then, too, the slowness of their introduction – which is attributable mainly to the repeated cuts in school building by the late George Tomlinson and Lady Horsbrugh – enabled political objections to be raised and the grammar schools (reorganized after the war) to become re-established with new staffs and new pupils. To establish a comprehensive school then created an outcry on behalf of an existing grammar school, as at Eltham Hill in 1953.

It would be unfair not to point out, too, that the experiment was tried on the poor but not on the well-to-do. I sat on the governing body of a comprehensive school whose chairman's son was a Wykehamist. It seemed ironical to take the grammar schools away from the poor but not to take Winchester away from a County Alderman's son.

But it is becoming clear that many comprehensive schools have been triumphant successes. In the absence of any comparative study it is impossible to say authoritatively whether they have helped the children of all abilities to mix more, and with fewer disadvantages, than any other system. But it must also be realized that they are rarely *socially* comprehensive, since the better-off almost always buy education, and that, except in Anglesey, the comprehensive schools exist everywhere alongside grammar schools. In this respect they resemble the more progressive, newly built, and excitingly run secondary modern schools.

The common school has recently been adopted in a number of European countries, and the evidence of its advantages has become considerable. In Sweden, for example, which has an academic tradition certainly not inferior to our own, there has been for the last ten years a movement towards the comprehensive school which has been so successful that it is now to become universal. In a carefully controlled experiment in which the city of Stockholm was divided into two, one half going over to the common school, while the other half remained divided into grammar schools and schools for children of lesser ability, the common schools have proved to be academically more successful with all groups of ability except, in the initial years, with boys of high ability from the working class. Even this group has now caught up, and it seems probable that their original retardation was due to the reorganization of the schools and the consequent disturbance of their academic careers rather than to the actual structure of the school system itself. Now that the common schools have become accepted there is no evidence that working-class boys of high ability are suffering any retardation.

It has even been demonstrated in Sweden that the

practice of dividing classes by ability within the common school is not always academically necessary, and the evidence from Norway suggests that it may even be undesirable. In these two countries the training of teachers has been designed to enable wide ranges of ability to be taught together, and the practice of 'setting' – that is to say, taking children of similar attainments in separate groups for different subjects – has been found to be a much more than adequate substitute for the rigid streaming which takes place in most English schools.

It may well be argued that Scandinavian experience is not relevant to England, although these countries have a strong intellectual tradition, and a social system which, although less snobbish, is not basically very different from our own. In the absence of detailed English evidence, however, the Scandinavian experience is the closest analogy that we have.

The arguments for a common secondary school are borne out to some extent at least by the impressionistic evidence that has been collected about the existing comprehensive schools in this country. Were we starting a school system afresh, there is no doubt in my own mind that, though we might later introduce differentiation for very handicapped or highly gifted children (as in the U.S.S.R. or the U.S.A.), we should start with common schools.

The present situation is, however, another case altogether. There are in existence many schools of all types which are, or consider themselves, successful. This applies especially to grammar schools. Many parents regard these schools as the best part of the public system. Their staffs, old boys and girls, parents, and pupils have hitherto resisted any attempt to 'abolish' them. It is true, of course, that they are a comparatively recent invention, that they have not always been so intellectually selective, and that many fail with their lowest streams, though one is also prepared to accept the major point that their intellectual and social tradition is a valuable one which many people prize.

Recently the introduction of comprehensive schools has been accelerated by deliberate ministerial decision. What we have to face is the situation as it is now, and as it will develop over the next decade. Let me point out certain facts. First, the adventitious criticisms of the modern schools – that they are relatively poorly housed, poorly equipped, and have staffs of low intellectual pretensions – are less and less relevant. As the schools are reorganized, and as new schools are built, there will be 'parity of equipment'. This will be quickly followed by a great increase in the number of graduate teachers. If these graduates are untrained it will be disastrous, of course; but if they are trained there will be little observable break in the continuum of qualification between the best grammar schools and the best modern schools. Further, as more and more children stay on to sixteen, seventeen, and eighteen, the differences will be further eroded. We know that many of the children in the modern schools are able to undertake sixth-form work with reasonable prospects of success. In such a situation the 11 plus will have become pointless, and (one may ask) what would then be the value of carrying on a battle about comprehensive schools – especially as it is extremely difficult to tell the difference between adjacent areas where one has a grammar school and a comprehensive school and the other a grammar school and a big modern school? So long as the schools are big enough to carry a varied and qualified staff (and 600 is surely the minimum for an effective secondary school) then any school can take its pupils to A level.

In all the arguments over the relative values of differing methods of education, the point to remember is that diversity in itself is excellent, provided that schools are not divided solely by intelligence or social class and that any specialization and streaming happens at as late an age as possible. It is preposterous that in a country of 54 million people one solution should alone be imposed, whether that solution be the bipartism which we have had, or a comprehensive system. There is room for variety. There is room for experiment in more and in less streaming by ability and attainment; there is room for more experiment in co-education, and for co-operation with industry and business in practical work. All this seems to me to add up to an argument for variety rather than uniformity, provided that we take steps to see that the range of ability recruited to any one school or type of schools is never narrow, for we know that tests of measured ability at any given age are very imperfect predictors of later educational performance.

This, and the other proposals I have outlined in this chapter, would help to lengthen the secondary-school career of the average child and would ensure that year by year the degree of selection of pupils by ability would rapidly decline. But this can only take place in a context in which the social exclusivism among the schools is being actively and rapidly reduced. This move towards greater social and intellectual comprehension will entail further changes in the training of teachers, so that teachers are able to understand the backgrounds and attitudes of working-class children more fully, and to acquire techniques which enable them to teach a wide variety of children in the same school. Such knowledge can be easily acquired, and for many years has been acquired, by those who teach in primary schools.

A necessary basis for this change has been the decision at national level, and in the majority of local authorities, to end the bipartite or tripartite secondary system. Various expedients are being adopted locally – wholly comprehensive as in London, a division at fourteen as in Leicestershire, a sixth-form college – but the national preference is for a single school. This is difficult to introduce because of the absence of purpose-built schools. Yet it is possible to run a school in two buildings, even when they are not on the same site, and to run comparatively small comprehensive schools. If the age of transfer is raised to thirteen, then a five-stream school (with 150 children in each age-cohort) would be no bigger than 750 children if all the children stayed at school until they were eighteen, and 600 if half of them left at sixteen. At the present rate of school building it is possible to foresee a widespread network of schools of this size, all over the country. The Circular issued in 1965 envisages some such solution, and it will be generally endorsed as experience broadens.

But let us not be too optimistic. The sources of social and educational handicap run very deep. They are to be found in the genetic make-up and environmental background of every child; and no school can do very much to overcome them. In the comprehensive schools the children from the good homes continue – by and large – to sweep all before them. I think that what the comprehensive school does is to remove, to some extent at least, the institutional barriers to a greater degree of academic fulfilment on the part of many children. So long as rigorous selection exists, many children are brought up short by a barrier created by society.

Given these policies there is no reason why there should not, by the end of the decade, be a wide range of secondary schools of high quality encouraging experiment in the subjects taught and in the ways in which they are taught, but not, as at present, rigorously divided by intelligence and social class.

The abolition of the greater part of such selection may well be a necessary basis for any major advances in teaching techniques. A further condition of such an advance is a reduction in the importance of external examinations; the procedure I have outlined for encouraging schools to assess their pupils, rather than allowing individual pupils to be assessed by external examinations, would perhaps be the most desirable single educational reform that could be undertaken in the near future.

The immediate result of such reforms would be a change (and an increase) in the number of boys and girls going on to the various institutions of higher education. How are we to cater for these new students?

CHAPTER SIX

HIGHER EDUCATION

IN comparison with other countries, the number of students in higher education in Great Britain – especially in England – is not large. In the United States, for instance, about a third of each age group go on to some form of higher education. Here it is probably about ten or more per cent, and in the plans for expansion which have so far been agreed this is not likely to rise above twenty per cent for ten years and thirty per cent in twenty years. What higher education we have is, moreover, divided and stratified in the most extraordinary way. On the one hand we have the universities which are expensive and well staffed, with students who are in general intensively taught. On the other hand there are technical colleges and colleges of education which on the whole do not teach for degrees, have comparatively few links with the universities, have low prestige and have been more or less strictly under the control of the local authorities or (in the case of some colleges) religious denominations, while getting their income from the Department of Education.

At present there are believed to be in the U.K. roughly 450,000 full-time students in higher education; in round figures, 230,000 in the universities, 110,000 in the colleges of education, and 100,000 in art schools, technical colleges, and polytechnics. There are probably 10,000 or more outside these clearly defined institutions who are full-time students.

Oxford and Cambridge, both about 10,000 students strong, once dominated the picture. Their prestige and influence is deservedly high, but their influence on other institutions may not be wholly to the good. Certainly, by setting standards of scholarship and independence and devotion to careful teaching (their failure rates are less than three per cent), they set a magnificent example. But by their very excellence they tend both to attract a high proportion of the best entrants, and to set a tone which other universities try to imitate. Because they are residential, it is felt that a proper university *should* be residential; because they have a tutorial system, with a moral responsibility for the students' welfare, it is felt that all universities should have this.

But other universities – those in Scotland and in the north of England – have a different sort of tradition. They are more adult, in one sense; and they are less inclined to believe in tutorial methods. The Scottish universities are ancient, and the Northern ones new – yet all tend to lay less emphasis on traditional subjects and more on newer ones, to emphasize student independence, to have a policy of professional government rather than a faculty and college structure. This tradition is now being broken. The very new universities look as though they will tend to emphasize the Oxbridge elements of the British university tradition rather than the civic university elements.

There is a similar dichotomy in the approach to students outside the universities. In colleges of education (which are mainly for girls) most of the students live in small colleges, where they are very intensively taught. The technical colleges (mainly for men), on the other hand, tend to be in the bigger towns, to have many students, and to have a less intensive teaching programme – probably because much of their work has to be done in the evenings and with part-time students spending most of their days at work. Here, again, the trend is now towards an Oxbridge pattern.

All these institutions of higher education are now expanding fast. It is important, therefore, to ask how big this expansion will be and what form it should take.

THE EXPANSION

By the end of the seventies there will be about 400,000 university students, over 100,000 in the training colleges and, say, 300,000 in other institutions of higher education. This makes a total of 800,000, or 200,000 new British students per year, which is well over twenty per cent of the age-group. Of these, well over half will be men. We are behind Canada (about twenty per cent) and the U.S. (about thirty per cent), and the plans in such European countries as France and Sweden are for proportions which will be somewhat higher than ours by 1980.

The pressures for expansion in higher education are very strong, and will get stronger. The first arises out of the wishes of the school-leavers themselves. A high proportion of those who leave school at eighteen wish to take part in higher education of some sort. The numbers of school-leavers with two A levels will rise rapidly. About thirty per cent of the school population at fourteen are in selective or independent schools. In the middle 1950s, sixty per cent of pupils from *independent* schools and twenty-four per cent of grammar-school pupils left at eighteen plus. By 1980 these percentages will be typical of all secondary schools.

Another pressure arises from the need of the economy for skilled man-power. The demand for school-teachers will probably require an increase in the annual rate of recruitment of between 10,000 and 20,000. This in itself implies an expansion of perhaps 60,000 to 70,000 places in higher education. The need for engineers, natural scientists, and other specialists will also increase. At the same time the ex-colonial territories will urgently require more places for their students here.

Yet another pressure springs from the increased needs of the professions for longer, more detailed training and stiffer conditions of entry. It is still the practice now, for example, for the majority af accountants, solicitors, surveyors, and similar professions to be recruited from sixteen- to eighteen-year-old school leavers, who prepare for their professional examinations by correspondence courses and evening classes. A rising proportion of these people, however, are taking degrees in economics, law, or estate management, and the growing professionalization in our country would suggest that there is a whole range of professions and sub-professions which will shortly be requiring two or three years of formal higher education as a condition of entry. Social work is a typical example of a career which has been professionalized in the last ten years, and which will make increasing demands upon the higher education system.

Thus it is certainly not unreasonable to suppose that by the 1990s there will be 200,000 to 250,000 people a year entering higher education, and that a million or so places will be a minimum requirement.

The expansion will therefore have to be a big one: an average minimum of five per cent a year for at least twenty years. However, in the next few years there is going to be an emergency. Because of shortage of funds, building has fallen behind, and there is continual pressure to find new places.

ORGANIZATION

The first major problem which arises is how to eliminate the present confusion in the structure, and to make a logical and orderly system under which the expansion can be rapidly pushed ahead. We must, in other words, construct machinery for the continuous coordination of higher education. This machinery is now organized by the Department of Education and Science. It has already led to a substantial improvement in the status of the former Ministry, and it is already making coordination of higher education with the needs of the schools and with the rise of further education much easier. The Secretary of State is already advised by the Schools Council for the Curriculum and Examinations, representing all the groups in higher education, the universities, technical colleges, and the schools, and this Council has a high degree of independence and autonomy. In addition the Department has a system now for long-term forecasting, for decisions in higher education are long-term ones. The relevant birth rate is twenty years before the entry, and the organization and structure of higher education is so complex and delicate that long-term views are essential.

At the moment the universities receive their grants from the University Grants Committee, which is run by a handful of permanent staff and itself consists of busy people sitting part time. The Committee is now being strengthened, and it is in a position to make much closer comparisons between universities of such things as building costs, research costs, student wastage rates, etc.; and it is becoming possible for it, under Mr Kenneth Berrill's chairmanship, to establish norms and to adopt far more positive long-term policies. This is a great improvement over the previous situation where the amateurishness and lack of leadership by the U.G.C. led to bad decisions, like the decision to use the quinquennium 1952–7 as a period of 'consolidation', when it could have been used by the universities and training colleges to produce the teachers of whose shortage we are now so acutely aware.

The universities have themselves established a Universities Central Council for Admissions (U.C.C.A.) which, together with the Clearing House for the Colleges of Education, is rationalizing the procedure for admission. This, together with the Schools Council's work on the relationship between schools and higher education, is reorganizing the whole process of admission to higher education – that is, the relationship between sixth-form work, undergraduate work and postgraduate work. For the effect of the previous lack of organization has been to push more and more work back into the schools, constantly increasing the pressure to specialize. (Grammar and public schools have always specialized, but that was because originally they chose to do so on educational grounds – largely represented in the Crowther Report – whereas they are not now free *not* to specialize.) To a number of people it seems right that the schools should at least be free to choose either to specialize or not. And in every other country, the general education of boys and girls is given priority. At the moment the universities in this country ask both for a general education and for deep specialist knowledge. They cannot in fact have both.

It is not a defence of 'academic freedom' to suggest that the right to demand impossibilities of the schools is a worthy aim of universities. Of course the universities can interview prospective candidates if they like, but to suggest that, in a situation where over 100,000 candidates from many thousands of schools are approaching several hundred centres of higher learning for admission, freedom of individual examination can be allowed to continue is a palpable absurdity. A universal school-leaving examination which was also used as an entrance examination, and which was not subject to any but the most broad limitations by faculty or type of institution, would be a charter of freedom for the schools. Better still, my proposal for the schools to choose their own students for higher education places would solve many problems. For then the problem would be one of assessing schools. This is a more worthwhile thing to do than to try to pick a few 'winners' (or some other racing metaphor). How would anybody assess a school? Partly on the quality of its education in general; partly on the quality of individual subjects; partly on the social background of its pupils. For a school with a good staff, a liberal view of education and pupils from a prosperous suburb, is bound to do 'better' in almost every sense, than a school staffed by transients, with no clear educational purpose, and drawing its pupils from an immigrant community (for the reasons I have given earlier). The basis for such an assessment exists in the reports of Her Majesty's Inspectors. The university departments of education could be called in to assist, and certain objective criteria established (of staff, pupils, buildings and equipment) which would form a basis for a rating – on a scale A to E – of schools; and candidates for different universities would be handicapped according to their school.

This is a job for the Schools Council. It, and the Department of Education and Science, have also to discuss the balance of faculties in the universities, and how it affects the schools. The machinery now exists, newly created, for consultation with many different institutions about admissions, degree courses, and standards.

Since an expansion of higher education on the scale now taking place will need (at least) a building programme of £100 million a year for twenty years, the control of costs and standards will have to be at least as comprehensive as that of the Department of Education. The teaching staff in higher education by 1980 might easily reach 80,000 (compared with the present 35,000); clearly salary negotiations and matters affecting conditions of service are now matters of considerable public importance.

Increasingly the growing volume of research in this country done in the universities is government sponsored, partly by the departments themselves, partly by the Science Research Council, the Social Science Research Council, the Medical Research Council and similar bodies. The coordination of this research effort is a major administrative problem; and the right policy to be adopted by the government towards the support of research has been much studied and investigated, both in this country and elsewhere. There is the possibility that too much applied research (and graduate work) will be advanced at the expense of the teaching of undergraduates; or, in both cases, the reverse might happen. For this reason the Department of Education and Science is a government department straddling both higher education and research, while the sponsoring of the more applied parts of research is left to departments like the Ministry of Technology, or the Ministry of Agriculture.

As higher education expands a number of the more familiar aspects of higher education are being subjected to further examination. Among the major decisions to be taken will be the place of residence in higher education. At present we are committed to the majority of our students living away from home. A similar proportion of a much larger number of students would be a heavy economic burden; and clearly questions of the use of such buildings (at present almost unoccupied for half the year) especially when a proportion of the students will be married, will be of great interest. It may well be that the use of these buildings in the vacations, for higher education of adults, is a real possibility which should be faced; certainly Sir Geoffrey Crowther was right to draw attention to the present prospect of an alarming waste of resources at a time when capital for productive investment is so scarce.

Another problem is that of maintenance grants for students; it is probable that the minimum maintenance for a student in 1980 will be £500 (at present prices), and this would involve outlays of £400,000,000 a year if the means test were abolished. Whether this will be possible is one question. Other questions are whether parents in our wealthier society might not help their own children far more than at present, and whether we ought not to rationalize the present situation where (despite what dons think) almost all students take paid work in the vacations. In America this work is found for them, and it is taken into account in assessing their scholarships.

Certainly there are ways and means by which higher

education can help to pay for its own expansion. In universities and colleges there is a strong case for improving the techniques of teaching, and for using modern technology for a lot of the work which is at present done by the use of very expensive man-power. There is a strong case for using some of the empty university buildings during the vacations by means of a shift system. There is a strong case for raising the pay of university teachers by encouraging them to do more teaching during the vacations, provided that this is not at the cost of their research and scholarship. This is a matter where investigation is needed, but it seems clear that many university teachers do not, in fact, spend anything like all their lengthy vacations on scholarship.

WHAT SHOULD BE TAUGHT, HOW, AND WHY

So far this chapter has been about the organization of higher education. What about its content? The crucial question is this: Should higher education be divided, as at present, into university and non-university institutions? Or put another way: What about 'university standards'?

I see no real problem in widening the scope of the universities so long as there is a rational division of labour, so that researchers and writers are not submerged by dreary routine and the great teachers are not handicapped by rigid syllabuses and unresponsive pupils. In a society with educational abundance it should be possible for people to be more free to teach what they want, in the way that they want, than they are at present. The sixth-form teacher is submerged by rigid A-level syllabuses; his freedom counts. And in a society where the chance of getting a degree is not as rare as it is now, it should be possible to find at least a minority of students who care for learning for its own sake. The pursuit of excellence – and that is really all that is worth pursuing – is actually inhibited by our present system designed for 'Very Superior People'.

If the universities were extended to cover the whole, or at least the greater part, of higher education there might at first be a drop in standards, but they would almost certainly improve all round in the long run.

This raises the question of academic self-government. At present the universities are far more free to take important decisions regarding their own welfare than school-teachers and other sections of higher education are. Here the government imposes its own changes by edict, as it has recently done in the case of teacher training. It is inconceivable that they could have done this to the least important university. What part ought teachers to play in running their own institutions? What is right, self-government or direct public control? Although this book is too short to analyse these problems, they exist, and must sooner or later be resolved.

What will be taught in the universities? They have at present two roles. One is to develop scholarship, and here graduate schools are bound to play an increasing part, with a stream of gifted and academically minded men and women entering them with aims and ambitions centred on scholarship (surely a more sensible word than 'research' with its connotations of silly theses on trivial subjects). The other role is to give a testing education to able people who will go on to take a high place in society – the 'Balliol function' it might almost be called. To fulfil this second role, the education they offer, like Greats, may often have to be broader than the present degree courses, and possibly longer.

At present they cater mainly for the academic high-flyers. Although a large number of the extra recruits to the universities will have at least as high ability as the undergraduates already there, a great many will be mainly the kind of people who now attend colleges of education or technical colleges. They will neither be capable of extremely advanced work, nor will they have the desire to do it. Furthermore, one of the aims of a reformed higher education system would be to reduce the pressure in the secondary schools where two or three subjects are developed to a very high level at the expense of the general education of the schoolboy or schoolgirl. Many headmasters and headmistresses would like their children to leave school having done five or six subjects to a level between O and A level, in a range chosen from both arts and science subjects, and with a broader background in music, literature, and modern languages than is often now the case. It could therefore follow that the level of attainment in any individual subject, even with children of high ability, at the age of eighteen, would be lower than it is now.

Consequently there may be a strong case for a preparatory year or two for most boys and girls going to universities which would correspond to the top of the present sixth forms. Possibly this could be in junior colleges. In some cases this preparatory period would be mainly a deepening of specialist knowledge in the subjects in which the honours degree was to be taken; but in other cases, particularly that of girls who wished to become teachers or social workers, or boys who were to become solicitors or accountants, there would be a strong argument for maintaining a high level of general education.

This preparatory year could take place either in the universities or in the existing boarding schools and colleges of education. It might well take place overseas, in Africa or Asia, or in the countries of the Common Market. There is no reason for example, why initially the whole of this age-group should not spend six months in France, Germany or Italy, acquiring an adequate working knowledge of these languages, while in return we extend hospitality to young people from these countries. It would certainly be no more expensive than many of our present arrangements, although it would raise problems of organization.

But after this initial year a choice has to be made. Either

we could push the study of vocational subjects intensively, as is done in the Soviet Union today, or we could try to delay vocational choice until a comparatively late stage. The argument for pushing vocational subjects is a strong one. The nation has a desperate need for skills of all kinds, and by the age of eighteen or nineteen many of these young people will be fairly certain of what they want to do and anxious to get down to what they regard as the serious work of their life.

But unfortunate consequences could follow from such a policy. One is that the existing universities have a prestige in our society which is on the whole denied to the other institutions of higher education, and this policy would run the risk of maintaining their prestige while the rest of higher education would follow broadly its present vocational pattern. We might create two classes as deeply divided as those of the public and the maintained schools today, and the vocational institutions might be strongly anti-educational in atmosphere. On the other hand, the giving of general education runs the risk of creating institutions with comparatively low academic standards, which are unable to maintain the zest and enthusiasm of good colleges – and certainly this is sometimes the case in America.

There are really three policies for the organization of higher education. The first is that proposed by the Robbins Committee; it was (briefly) that there should be fifty or so universities (compared with our present forty-five in Great Britain) and that these should form the major part of higher education. Some of the universities would be high-prestige technological universities formed from the ten existing colleges of advanced technology; these colleges have, in fact, been given university status. Some of the colleges of technology would have been given special high-prestige status as S.I.S.T.E.R.s, Special Institutions of Technological Education and Research, as they were to have been called. This proposal has been rejected by the Government.

The colleges of education were to become constituent parts of the universities receiving their finance from the Government through the University Grants Committee and the universities themselves, and eventually forming part of the degree-giving institutions. The other technical colleges were to be largely left on one side under the aegis of the local education authority. They were to be able to give degrees through a National Council of Academic Awards (the N.C.A.A.). This body has in fact been set up under the chairmanship of Lord Kings Norton. The Government has rejected the proposals about teacher training colleges although it hopes that the academic links with the universities which have developed since 1945 particularly will be strengthened. It has insisted, however, that during the period of acute teacher shortage it is essential for the teacher training colleges to be directly under the influence of the Department of Education and Science, without the double buffer of the U.G.C. and the universities between them.

Thus the Government has adopted a half-way house between the Robbins Committee and what might be called a full-scale binary system. This is that there should be on the one hand a university system much as at present, and on the other hand a full-scale system concerned with professional and vocational education (largely on the model of the American Land Grant Universities). This would attempt to raise the prestige of vocational studies in this country without in any way distorting them by academicizing them. Thus if we were fully to support the binary system there is no doubt that the incorporation of the technological universities into the university system on the scale that it has been done has weakened the case for arguing that the second system, based upon the technical colleges, is as strong as the first system based upon the universities. Further, the incorporation of the greater part of teacher training into the vocational sector would be essential and would be resented.

The third possibility is that the whole of higher education should be incorporated into the university sector, and that the university sector should lose the considerable degree of independence that it at present enjoys. It would need, of course, to be administered with due precautions for maintaining academic freedom, but, in principle, decisions on building, the scale and size of the recruitment to different faculties, and the balance of research, would be taken regarding the system as a whole. In fact it seems inevitable that the eventual paths of British higher education will be a compromise between this system and the present binary system. When the technical colleges and the colleges of education have been built up during the period of great expansion which is now going on there will eventually be in Great Britain something like 400,000 students in them and something like 400,000 students in the existing and projected universities. The university system will be mainly academic in its bias, while the other system will be mainly vocational in its emphasis. But the division will be a blurred one, and it is possible to foresee a situation in which institutions of very high prestige are to be found in both systems.

In this context the development of the National Council of Academic Awards is of tremendous importance, because it will be validating the courses of a very large number of separate institutions. It is difficult to resist the conclusion that so great will be its work that it will be forced to become a series of regional bodies. If it becomes a series of regional bodies then the way is open for true Land Grant Universities in this country based upon regional institutions. For example, all non-university institutions in Berkshire, Buckinghamshire and Oxfordshire might very well become component parts of a local university of Oxfordshire, Berkshire and Buckinghamshire, which would have a substantial number of students on each of its campuses which would be mainly centred in Reading, Aylesbury, High Wycombe and

Oxford; while at the same time there would be two more or less autonomous universities at Reading and at Oxford.

This corresponds quite closely to the scheme that was proposed in the Labour Party Report under Lord Taylor presented to the nation just before the Robbins Report.

It is possible to foresee a flexible pattern of higher education maintaining high standards, adequate to service our society with technical skills, and giving opportunities for higher education to all of those who are both prepared for it and need it. But it would raise considerable problems of organization and finance. One major problem is how to maintain the independence of the universities once they have expanded to include so much of a much bigger system of higher education, without, at the same time, making them unresponsive to the needs of the society of their time. For example, a sudden switch in the demand for engineers might entail considerable changes in university courses. How could this be imposed on the universities without denying them their essential freedom in ordering their curricula?

A second problem is that the finance will have to come largely from the government. I have argued that, by the use of new techniques and by encouraging students to work productively during the vacations, much of the present expenditure could be kept within reasonable limits. Nevertheless, between £400,000,000 and £500,000,000 a year will certainly be spent on higher education by 1980. This is a great deal of money, and will have to be provided in the main by the taxpayer. In addition, the costs of scientific research are continually rising, and it would certainly be the hope of most distinguished scientists that the greater part of scientific research should be done either in the universities or in very close association with them. So far no effective study has been made of the way in which this could be financed.

Finally, there is the major problem of stratification and quality. At present there is a hierarchy in higher education, from Oxford and Cambridge at the top down to the smallest teacher-training college at the bottom, which corresponds fairly closely to the hierarchy in the schools from Eton and Winchester down to the secondary modern schools, and to the hierarchy which exists in business and in the professions. Many would claim that the significant division is no longer that between the public schoolboy and the rest, but that between those who went to Oxford or Cambridge and those who did not. Is there any prospect of reducing this distance?

A number of proposals have been put forward that Oxford and Cambridge should become graduate universities. It seems highly probable that in common with the other universities, this is likely to be the tendency. The proportion of graduates in the universities has risen greatly since the war, and seems likely to go on rising. It might well be that it would be typical for a young man or woman to leave school, go for a year to a general introductory course at one of the ex-public schools, take a degree at a university, and then go on for graduate work to one of the six or seven major centres like London, Manchester, Oxford, or Cambridge. This would be a close approximation to the American system. It is difficult to believe that the hierarchy in higher education could be maintained exactly as it is at present in conditions of very rapid expansion. There will be so many new subjects, and so many exciting new developments which – if only because of their size and cost – will take place outside Oxford and Cambridge, that the relative prestige of these universities is in many respects bound to decline. This will not be the result of a conscious attack on their standards from a passion for egalitarianism, but rather of the growing complexity of the criteria by which institutions of the university type will be judged.

It must be remembered that this country does not live in a world all by itself. In the university sphere, no less than in

81

industry, we are in direct competition with institutions overseas, especially in the United States. In so far as we try to achieve a drab uniformity of standards in all our institutions of higher education, so we are far more likely to lose our best people and to fall behind in research and learning, compared with the United States. If Oxford were to be reduced to the status of a local technical college, the people who left it would not go to some northern university, but rather to Harvard, Michigan, or the University of California. This is a most important point. It is particularly important to remember too that Oxford and Cambridge are the most successful institutions for the teaching of undergraduates that this country has ever seen. There is a very strong case, therefore, for building them up, together with some other major universities on an international scale, and it was part of the unfortunate tone of the Robbins Report that it apparently ignored this.

APPRENTICESHIP AND ADULT EDUCATION

There is another aspect of education which will change during the next ten years, and it is already possible to see how the change will take place. It has become customary for something like one-third of the young male entrants to employment to be apprenticed to their occupation. On the whole this system of apprenticeship has become ill-adapted to the purpose which it is supposed to serve. In many instances there are very few formal arrangements for the apprentice to learn his skill. He picks it up under the casual supervision of craftsmen who are not trained to teach. He takes a great many years to learn his trade – sometimes as many as seven – and the course is extremely wasteful of his time and energy. In many cases the greater part of two or three years is spent as tea boy or general messenger. There is little attempt to see that the craft or skill which is being acquired is related to fundamental scientific and engineering principles, so that it becomes difficult for the skilled man later to adapt himself to new techniques.

It is exceedingly difficult for progress to be made from an apprenticeship to any other level of education. There is a part-time system of education leading to ordinary national certificates and higher national certificates, which is given partly through evening courses, partly through day release, and partly through sandwich courses, but investigations have revealed that a great deal of this education is ill-organized, that the vast majority of those who take part in it leave without attaining the qualifications for which they were entered, and that, compared with full-time education, it is extremely expensive in the time of teachers and taught. Furthermore, the relationship between the apprentice and those who teach him is based on private arrangements, either through the individual firm or the individual industry, and there is no national scheme to make provision either for those who enter firms with no such arrangements for training or for industries which are so ill-organized that they are unable to provide themselves with the skills which are necessary in modern competition.

The Industrial Training Act provides a major breakthrough in this field. The Industrial Training Council and the Boards which report to it, which have been set up for the major industrial groups, are imposing levies on firms throughout the country from which they are supporting training schemes, including approved training schemes in the firms themselves. The aim of this scheme is the rapid improvement of industrial training schemes and the provision of training schemes where so far there are none. It marks, in fact, the end of the apprenticeship system as it has been known in this country. Two major developments may be foreseen; in fact this is the way in which part-time further education will become compulsory, because it is most probable that the training schemes approved by the Boards will include provision as part of their courses, for compulsory day release.

The second thing which is very important is that increasingly the Boards will be forced either to provide training facilities themselves or to make use of further education facilities provided by the local authorities. This will require a complete reconsideration of the existing system of further education.

By and large industry is not providing itself with the expert technicians that it needs, except in the isolated instances of a few large firms and some of the nationalized industries. At the present rate of labour turnover, a firm often finds that it has trained people at great expense only to lose them to its competitors. It is therefore incumbent upon the Government to provide a general level of skill and training over and above that which industry provides. It is also quite clear that this training in high technical ability should be financed by industry, through a compulsory levy, for until the Act, the bad and inefficient firms were gathering the benefits provided by the good and efficient firms who took care to train their young workers thoroughly. This technical educational training must be closely related to fundamental knowledge in the sciences, technology, and in the arts of communication, especially in English and mathematics.

The idea of the county college, which was to provide part-time education for secondary modern school-leavers, is by itself an empty concept unless it is linked closely to the working needs of the nation. But once it is based upon the fundamental acquisition of skills it could become an extremely important part of the education system.

LEISURE

There is too another aspect of further education which is no less important. The nation at present is divided in two in its leisure time. The child who receives an academic education is offered the full range of athletic, musical, dramatic, artistic, and other facilities within the school itself, until he is eighteen. Then at university or training college he will expect to be provided with playing fields, halls with stages, gymnasia and unions, and all the other facilities which seem to those of us brought up in an academic environment to be perfectly normal accompaniments of education. Until comparatively recently the non-academic child has had none of these things at school, and it is only with the school building programme of the middle and later fifties that the secondary modern schools have come to be provided with gymnasia and playing fields on anything like the scale the grammar schools have been used to. Even now there is still a big gap to be made up.

But from fifteen years onwards the non-academic child who has left school has a ludicrously small provision for his leisure activities in comparison with those offered to his more academic contemporary. Thus at the universities membership of the Union, acres of playing fields, and an experimental theatre are all subsidized by the exchequer from public maintenance grants, whereas boys and girls in the heart of large cities are, at best, provided only with youth clubs and Outward Bound courses. There seems in principle no reason why the facilities of undergraduates should not be provided for the whole population of this age-group as of right, and there can be little doubt that such provision would revolutionize the leisure activities of those who have left school early.

But to enjoy leisure they need more leisure time. It is somewhat ironical to think that the middle class continually congratulates itself on the amount it works, when it is recalled that the typical skilled or semiskilled worker works from 8 a.m. to 5 p.m. and may very well work overtime, often in conditions of extreme physical unpleasantness. Those who were educated at Oxford or Cambridge will recall that the afternoons were customarily left free – for games or punting, or reading or talking. To provide the same facilities for youth in industry would mean a substantial reduction in working hours.

If this were done, there seems in principle no reason why working youth should not enjoy the same benefits as its academically more successful contemporaries. Thus one can conceive a two-pronged attack on the years from sixteen to twenty-one of the less academic children, which will provide them with apprentice training in a way closely related to the fundamental principles of education, and give the same sort of environment for leisure pursuits which has been up to now reserved for the more fortunate members of their age-group.

ADULT EDUCATION

Having made this substantial advance one final gulf in society will reveal itself. For those going through education already, or those who are about to do so, there has been a substantial rise in standards. It is true that this rise is uneven, but it cannot be denied that it has taken place, or, given adequate arrangements and expenditure, that it is likely to accelerate. This leaves behind, however, in the older generation of society, the products of the inadequate education system which we have hitherto suffered.

The man who retired in 1960 first went to school in 1900, a time when classes were very large, a third of the children were verminous, and the school-leaving age was still thirteen. These conditions, of course, did not prevail when the great majority of young adults were at school, but almost a third of the population still left school before the enactment of the 1944 Education Act, and the great majority before its implementation in any serious sense. It is no less necessary for them to be prepared to change their jobs, to acquire new skills, to make harmonious relationships with their families, to make their contributions to society, to travel and enjoy themselves than it is for young people. It is for this reason that the adult-education system exists, provided partly by the local authorities and partly by such bodies as the Workers' Education Association. This system not only helps those who wish to learn specific subjects, those, for instance, who feel the need to develop a foreign language, but also provides courses which enable people to enjoy their lives more fully.

The most fruitful field for the development of adult education is the use of television and the radio. Already a great deal is done by the B.B.C. and some of the commercial television companies, but it is doubtful whether it has yet been fully understood how effective these media could be in promoting a sustained education effort.

The idea of the Open University, which the Government has adopted and which was so strenuously promoted by the National Extension College, is a most exciting development of this kind, and together with the courses provided by the correspondence colleges, there is no doubt that a serious effort in adult education on a completely new scale can be developed through the use of the new media.

The growth of universities and new forms of education is part of a shift upwards in the age limits of education for all. In the next twenty or thirty years we can expect to see twenty, thirty, or forty per cent of an age-group going on to some sort of course after the age of eighteen. But this will lead to a growing division between those with advanced skills and those without them unless we adopt as a general principle the notion that up to twenty-one everyone is fundamentally the responsibility of the education service and can be employed only if that employment is beneficial to the young worker as well as useful to the economy. One of the myths of our time is that the young worker is the pampered child of the Welfare State. This is not so. The majority come from ugly towns and mean homes, and work in unattractive conditions. It is rather pointless giving good primary schools to the children if something is not done about this.

But, as in so much else, everything in the schools depends upon there being enough teachers of the right kind. Will there be?

CHAPTER SEVEN

THE TEACHERS

MORE – AND DIFFERENT – TEACHERS

All our efforts in education depend on teachers. Their position in our society is a strange one; their status is anomalous. Are they the worst-paid profession, or the best-paid skilled workers? Are they a profession at all?

In this chapter I will argue that the teachers are changing – they are quite different now from what they were twenty years ago. Because of this, they need more pay; they need better training; and above all they need professional self-government. It seems to me that at present, amidst all the comings and goings, a new attitude is developing which will make the teachers a powerful force. One day somebody will capitalize their search for status and for pay into a demand for professional self-government. The teachers will tread the doctors' path.

In the old days the way of escape for the clever poor boy or girl was to teach. By becoming a pupil teacher he could rise from the manual working class. Many of those who did became apostles of standards which they had themselves attained. They tried passionately to change their pupils, and to rescue the clever ones from a life of drab toil. Confronted day by day with material and spiritual poverty, their own lives a witness to the efforts needed to rise from it, they were inescapably revolutionaries in spirit. The 1945 revolution began in large part in the classroom.

After the war there was a large influx of very good men from the forces, through the Emergency Training Colleges, but there has been a change since then. For some, especially for girls, teaching is now a soft option. It is easy to become trained, easy to get a job, and the rewards are adequate, if not high. Teachers regard themselves as middle-class and some have adopted the myth of the contemporary middle class that life for them is hard and their rewards small, while for many of their pupils and their parents life is abundant, careless, and easy. This is an exaggeration, of course. Many teachers do not feel this; and it is true that life, for some boys and girls, is a plethora of worldly goods. But one has an uncomfortable feeling that the essential truth is there. Teachers have become a conservative force. None so ready as they to accept the safe and conventional view; none so quick to criticize trade unions; none who enjoy the Young Conservative tennis parties more than some young primary-school teachers.

The effects of this on English life are incalculable. One thing that can be seen as a sure result is that the training of teachers must change profoundly. The people coming forward to be trained are different from their predecessors. As a general rule they are better educated; their top echelons are indistinguishable from undergraduates not only in intelligence but also in attainment. They are coming into a world, too, where teaching is not, as it once was, the summit of their ambitions: only a few years back it was a well-paid, safe, respectable job, differing in all these respects from their fathers' manual or semi-skilled insecurity. Teaching is now only one of a myriad of jobs much alike in pay, status, and cleanliness.

Further, graduates used to be a tiny and respected minority in a large profession. Already they are a fifth of the total working in maintained schools and colleges; by 1980 they will be a high proportion of the new entrants; by 1990 they may well be a majority of the profession. It is inevitable that most of the male secondary teachers will be graduates. There will be a number in the primary schools. (I am not now discussing whether this is *desirable*; I am saying it is inevitable.) Indeed, the biggest single change in the teaching profession is the increase in its size. And we need more teachers – quickly.

The rate of growth of the teaching force has been

substantial since the end of the war. In 1947 there were about 230,000 teachers in England and Wales in all schools (public and private); in 1967 there were 370,000 teachers. The rate of recruitment has varied annually, changing as the number of ex-servicemen who came into teaching after the war were absorbed, and then from year to year as the number of products of the training colleges and universities became available for teaching.

It seems likely that over the next twenty years at least another 250,000 teachers will be needed, and this represents a net annual rate of recruitment of 12,500 a year, or (in gross terms) probably about 50,000 new recruits to the profession each year for the foreseeable future. In the short run the scarcity of teachers is likely to grow more acute in that the rapid increase in the number of pupils at school, which has only just stopped, took place at the same time as a rapid efflux of young married teachers recently recruited. There are signs, however, that this efflux may be slowing down and the rate of recruitment of married women teachers is showing signs of increasing. A number of short-term measures have been adopted by the Department of Education and Science to accelerate the recruitment of teachers. This includes a crash training programme by the opening of annexes to colleges of education, the rapid expansion of training colleges, and special inducements for the recruitment of married women by the local authorities. There is evidence that by bold and imaginative policies the worst of the crisis has been averted. Taking one year with another, now it is possible to foresee a big annual increase. This rate will be affected by several major forces. One is the size of the higher education system. Over a third of those who are produced by higher education take up teaching, and it is virtually impossible to raise this proportion significantly without starving other occupations of the trained people they need. Consequently, there can be enough teachers in the schools only if the higher-education system grows very rapidly indeed. This will have to be accompanied, as I shall explain below, by arrangements for training teachers, but the basic problem remains that of providing sufficient places in higher education.

The changing status of women is the second major problem in recruiting teachers – a problem exacerbated by the high rate of marriage among women teachers. Two out of every three teachers retiring today are young women leaving either to marry or to have children. We now have earlier marriage and larger families, which may mean that the overwhelming majority of young women recruits to the teaching profession will spend a period of from five to ten years, from the middle twenties to the early thirties, at home, and in part the size of the profession depends on whether or not these women are prepared to return to the schools.

The majority of teachers will always be women. Among them the graduates are likely to be in a minority. The greater number will come from the colleges of education, where the ratio of women to men is three to one. They will be the products of three-year courses. But once they begin teaching most of them will stop within a year or two, become full-time wives and mothers for anything up to ten years, and then return to teaching.

There has been of course a revolution in the status of women, but their position as dependants during at least ten years of their adult lives – given present social arrangements – seems unavoidable. It seems inevitable, too, that the men teachers will be expected to make a career of their profession, whereas the number of women who will, from the age of twenty or twenty-two, look forward to almost forty years of uninterrupted teaching – which is at present almost a *sine qua non* of reaching the highest levels – will be small. Thus a change in the social status of teaching is dependent upon, and implies, a change in the social status of women.

THE TEACHERS

Social status depends – in part at least – on pay. In recent years the teachers have become more militant in their demand for more money. They are scarce and they know it.

Now pay and quality are very closely connected; so is respectability and the absence of strikes. The teachers are in a state of total confusion because it is agreed that they should have more pay and status – yet, in an economic framework set by the urgent necessity to control prices and incomes, the circumstances are against them. What can be done about this?

One basic difficulty is that there is now, since 1945, a basic salary scale which is identical for men and women, and for all trained teachers, whether or not they are graduates. Additional allowances are paid for degrees and other qualifications, and for posts of responsibility, such as head-teacherships, but in essence the difference between the lowest-paid newest entrant with the lowest qualifications and the most senior members of the profession is narrower in education than in many other jobs, and certainly the difference in pay is comparatively small between typical teachers in grammar and primary schools. This leads to dissatisfaction in some teachers at the top, but any attempt to help them upsets those at the bottom and gives further ground for disputes.

There is very little evidence that the rate of recruitment to the profession as a whole has been reduced by the pay-scales which have been in force for the last few years. It is generally true to say that, for women, teaching is the most attractive and best-paid occupation which they may freely enter – and the same may be true for the less well qualified men.

For the more highly qualified possessors of scarce skills such as mathematics and physics, however, teaching represents an exceptionally poor choice, and for this reason there has been a noticeable decline in the professional qualifications of those who teach these subjects in the sixth forms. On economic grounds alone, therefore, there is a strong case for paying more to first-class graduates in science subjects. But the case for paying more to other members of the teaching profession is now a strong one. The recent strikes prove this. There has been a noticeable shift in recent years towards improving the conditions offered in private employment compared with those in public employment. The public services were formerly alone in offering security of tenure, dignity of work, and adequate superannuation. They have now been overtaken in many cases by private employers. An expansion of education of the order that we must envisage implies a demand for teachers which is likely to rise faster than the supply, and economic analysis suggests that the teachers will be in a very strong position to improve their relative standing in the labour market.

There is, however, another side to the question. It has long been customary for economists of a *laissez faire* persuasion to pour scorn upon the notion that individuals should be paid what they are 'worth'. It has been pointed out that an individual's income measures his scarcity in the productive process, and that it is quite impossible on moralistic or *a priori* grounds to assign people a position in the earning hierarchy without disrupting the economy. Of recent years this has seemed less and less true. The labour market works most inefficiently, and the social values which appear to be implicit in the present structure of earnings are strongly contrary to those of a society which is concerned above all to raise its general standards.

The Burnham Committee in its traditional form came to an end because the nation had to have a wages policy. This is desirable if we are to have economic growth without rising prices. But it means that in future we have to take decisions about salaries and wages on avowedly social as well as economic grounds. Now a rise in the relative status of teachers in our society would entail a big rise in taxation, as it would necessarily be accompanied by a rise in the payments to other public servants. It is, therefore, only possible to foresee a substantial shift in the relative position of teachers in the earning hierarchy in a situation in which a completely revised system of settling incomes has been established. There is little doubt that at some time in the foreseeable future a complete re-casting of the national incomes situation will occur. But until this does it is difficult to see how the teachers can make a noticeable advance in the incomes hierarchy. Thus, once more, education is seen to take its part in a wider social argument, and the position and social status of teachers to depend on fundamental changes in social organization.

TRAINING

Teaching is always changing, even if only slowly and incoherently. To begin with, the whole pattern of teacher training is altering. At present most students enter a three-year teacher-training course at eighteen. The colleges used to be predominantly residential, fairly small (less than 500) and often single-sexed – which means they were mainly for girls. Conditions are less authoritarian than they were – doors locked at 10 pm, no male visitors and so on – but they are still in some colleges not wholly appropriate to the status of a 'student', with all the freedom and independence the term implies. Rapid changes have, however, taken place. The rapid growth of the colleges of education (the number of students in them will have multiplied over a period of twenty years by over four times) means that the typical college will be at least a thousand students strong. They will be mixed because the number of men students has been increasing as a deliberate consequence of public policy. They are much more closely linked academically to the universities than they used to be.

The standard both of staff and students has noticeably improved and the introduction of the three-year course a few years ago has enabled a significant improvement in the academic conditions of the colleges to take place.

The students study a mixture of general subjects (English, mathematics, social studies), a subject they will specialize in (English for example), and 'educational' subjects – psychology, sociology, and philosophy. Much of this last seems to be on a pretty poor level, especially the 'philosophy', but it is linked in a continuous process of practice in teaching, visits to schools and so on, which is admirably done. In contrast to the more formal subjects, where the amount of lecturing may at times be excessive and the studying wooden, the 'pedagogics', as the practical teaching side might be called, is alive and interesting. It capitalizes on the interest of young women in children, and the concern of most young people to 'get on with the job' – which much of the rest of our education seems designed to postpone to as late as possible with unhappy results. Thus, whatever reforms are proposed in training, the vocational content of the courses should be developed and strengthened.

For graduates, training is already the responsibility of the universities. They follow a one-year course, which is sometimes praised, but often heavily criticized as too theoretical and of poor intellectual quality. The objections are not entirely valid. There is a real problem in teaching people about children and schools when their instincts are to teach as they were themselves taught, and the schools they go to (especially grammar and public schools) are wary of 'new' methods and approaches. Nevertheless, a number of people have advocated a greater degree of 'apprenticeship' for graduates. They would be posted to schools where the staff would be trained to help them; and the tutors in the university department of education would organize the course at the university in close relation to the experience in the schools.

In some respects this is, in fact, exactly what is done now; the innovation would be to regularize the relationship with the schools, to adapt the salary structure and to formalize the two-year apprenticeship. Certainly some changes will be required when training becomes compulsory – as it must be – because it is only through a properly organized training scheme that modern techniques of teaching and new attitudes are introduced into the schools.

In the long run, of course, we cannot say that a situation in which the teaching profession is divided into graduates, as the term has been commonly understood hitherto, and non-graduates can be allowed to persist. If the rate of progress of the colleges of education is as fast as it has been there is little doubt that not only will a proportion of their students take a new kind of degree, a Bachelor of Education, but that many of them will be able to take existing Honours and general degrees at the universities. The time has surely come when we should press strongly for the whole teaching profession to be a graduate profession. This would mean that those people with the requisite school-leaving qualifications, who enter colleges of education and take the three- or four-year course there, should be granted a degree at the successful conclusion of their studies. It is far less important what this degree is labelled than that they should have a degree. The integration of the teaching profession depends very strongly upon the elimination of the division between graduates and non-graduates.

If this is one essential step towards an effective and satisfactory job for teachers, there is another which is less obvious but no less essential.

PROFESSIONAL SELF-GOVERNMENT

As I pointed out earlier, the position of teachers in our society has always been an anomalous one. They have only recently risen from a low social status, and in the past they were mostly women without specific qualifications. Today more and more of them are graduates, but as a professional body they are not yet as well organized as doctors are.

In the National Health Service the doctors are represented by statute on almost all boards and committees. On some they are in a majority. The strength of the professional representatives *vis-à-vis* the lay members is enhanced both by the prestige of the doctors and by the appointed nature of the laymen who can speak for none but themselves and have to be careful not to offend the appointing body. The power of the medical profession is perhaps best seen in the hospital service, where the influence of laymen is in some respects less than it has ever been before. This springs largely from the fact that the laymen no longer provide the finance, which they did as benefactors to the voluntary hospitals and as councillors in the local authority hospitals.

There is a striking contrast in education. The teachers are represented on the central advisory committees, and they are usually represented on local education committees or divisional executives by a few co-opted members. On some advisory committees of divisional executives they are in a majority. But they are hardly ever represented directly on school governing bodies, where the only professional person usually present is the head teacher, who has the right to attend but has no vote, and occasionally an inspector. The 400,000 teachers are mainly appointed by lay people; their conditions of service are determined in negotiation with employing authorities of lay people; and their professional lives are to some extent controlled by inspectors appointed locally and centrally. As has been said, some of the weakness of the teachers as a professional body compared with doctors and dentists springs from the lack of respect in which their profession has been held by the general public. Compared with doctors their social origins have been lowly; there are proportionately many more women; and their average academic qualifications are less. Much of their weakness, however, arises from the use of local authorities as the controlling bodies, which has made it inevitable that professional membership of committees can only be by co-option and that ultimate power must rest with the elected body because it votes the necessary finance.

Self-government is an index of professional status. As the University Grants Committee wrote in 1921 about university lecturers in a section labelled 'Status': 'It appears to us imperative that the lecturers should be given an effective voice in internal administration'; and again in 1923: '... the sooner university teachers can be given some experience of administrative problems the better it will be for a university.'

It has not yet been asked – though it surely should have been – which of these two courses is the right one for a social service to take. What are the advantages of a high degree of professional representation as of right?

It is common knowledge that in the National Health Service professional representation on this scale was the price that had to be paid for such cooperation as was given by the doctors in inaugurating the service. Moreover, the consultants saw that the right path was to seek power first and pay would afterwards follow, whereas so far the teachers have trod the more working-class, trade-union path of a demand for pay and not for self-government. One advantage of professional representation is that it involves a profession in a discussion of public interest as well as its own. Once a profession is given the task of administration, the cold war between bureaucrats and workers in the field tends to become an internecine struggle. This is a social gain because it means that administration becomes less rigid, less bureaucratic, if only because it is more acceptable. Administration is also more effective. Previously committees have tended to include one solitary expert, to whom the other members have all deferred on technical points, but if more professional people were to join such committees the power of the single expert would be diminished.

Giving as many people as possible some control over their daily lives diffuses power, which is a good thing. A profession gives status to a group of people and in return the public are entitled to expect certain standards of behaviour. In return for control, responsibility must be accepted. This is not, of course, to say that the teachers should have so much power that they could give themselves jobs, hide their own misdemeanours, spend public money without accounting for it except through a formal approval of some executive decision, or behave irresponsibly. But these points must always be borne in mind when discussing the handing over of greater power to a professional body.

But all professions are dependent upon other professions; each of us is a seller of labour and a purchaser of labour's products. Political society has always been a settlement of conflicting interests. The strengthening of any profession, therefore, is not necessarily a reduction in the power of the public interest, but of the interest of other professions. In the mass anonymity of modern society the sense of belonging to a group is one of the means by which the individual redresses the balance against the mastery of the community over all his actions. People belong to several groups – the family, their profession, their club or hobby – and in all these ways power is diffused through society. If we look at the growth of one group we may see a falling-off of the power of society as a whole; if we look at society as a whole we see a diffusion of power because of the great growth of interest groups. In an age of complex technology the power of the expert is great. A profession gives responsibility to that power, and the growth of other professions emphasizes the situation of mutual dependence in which we all live.

To the teachers we give enormous possibilities of influence while denying them the actual exercise of administrative power. For no weapon is more devastating than the forming of a child's mind, and the teachers are given virtually absolute discretion in that aspect of their work. It would be hard to argue that their exercise of that influence has been other than disinterested and enthusiastic – whatever views one might hold about the nature and success of modern teaching. It seems, therefore, the height of absurdity to give a teacher the power to teach many children the difference between right and wrong, truth and untruth, seemly and unseemly behaviour, while at the same time we deny him the authority to help choose his colleagues or plan the provision for education in his area except in a largely advisory capacity.

There is a further issue – the division of power between parents and teachers. In universities the teachers have absolute control. In schools, the politicians and the administrators have the whip hand. Often, the parents feel that their interests are neglected. They are represented by neither party. It is important that the primary social unit, the family, should be given due weight. This is a genuine argument for tempering the power of the teaching profession. In this instance the parent is a particular example of the citizen-consumer. His interests are, in general, sovereign, and professional power must be subordinate to them. On the other hand, a flat uniformity is just what we seek to avoid. In these circumstances a difficult choice must be made. In education the deciding factor is that the decisions which have to be taken, and which benefit the parents, must have the support of the teaching profession if they are to be implemented in full and, because any change must involve the cooperation of the profession, we have to involve the teachers from the very beginning in the initiation and guidance of the change. Under existing conditions this involvement has often not occurred. The teachers – as far as can be seen from the statements of their organizations, and from private conversation – often do not trust the local authorities.

In short, in this chapter I have argued that the kind of person who becomes a teacher now is different from his predecessor, and therefore requires a different form of training; that the old trade-union attitude to pay is obviously ineffective; and that one of the major ways of improving the status of the teachers is to give them more professional self-government. This will lead to more pay.

Since the financial changes in education will necessarily require a far greater degree of central government and finance, it seems well worth looking next at the whole structure of local government to see whether it is any longer appropriate to the times. A full-scale investigation of local authorities is now under way. What place will education have in a new local authority structure?

CHAPTER EIGHT

ADMINISTERING EDUCATION

AT present the theory is that local authorities run education within broad lines laid down by Parliament and interpreted by the Department. The teachers – especially the head teachers – decide what actually goes on in the schools, guided by the advice of Her Majesty's Inspectors and the local inspectorate. At local county borough and county council elections the people decide what sort of education they want locally. The result is a rich variety, a diversity that leads to experiment and democratic strength.

Some of this is true, but most of it is less true than it was. The power of the Department has grown enormously in recent years. They are the source of the money, the policies, the ideas. Indeed, more and more people expect a national policy in education; when they move from Wigan to Wakefield they are shocked to find differences. And more and more there is a growing national debate about education.

At the same time the teachers have become stronger and resent the power of local councillors and others to 'interfere'. Finally the parents, as parents, are at last beginning to feel they should have choice – and choice means a say in what goes on at school.

These three forces – the Department, the teachers, and the parents – represent a new balance, quite different from that laid down in the 1944 Act. While it is true that some of the local authorities have been great initiators, others have not. London's comprehensive schools, Hertfordshire's architecture, Reading's experimental secondary schools, the West Riding's primary schools, and Leicestershire's flexible secondary-school system are deservedly well known. In the main, however, it is probable that as much of the impulse for change comes from the Department, in its monolithic building in Curzon Street, as from local authorities. It would be wrong to pretend that only good came out of Curzon Street (which single-handedly imposed the bipartite division of secondary schools on the country under the Attlee Government), but the logic of the situation results in the money and the ideas being more and more concentrated there.

This is inevitable with the rise in expenditure – a rise which will require a complete reform of the finance of education. By 1970 we were spending £2,200 million a year. By 1980 it should probably be at the rate of £3,000 million (all at 1970 prices). The present structure is inappropriate for this, since education finance is partly tied to the rates, and this means that a great service undergoing a rapid expansion is handicapped by an inelastic tax which falls relatively more heavily on the poor than on the rich. The arguments are strongly in favour of *raising* the proportion of expenditure met by the Government. New taxes might be levied – one on the employment of people aged sixteen to twenty-one and one on industry for the use of skilled workers. We need experiment. But if central finance increases, central control is likely to increase too. In this situation, how far can local authorities be used to develop education?

Many have been excellent in the past, some have been bad. The trend is towards a demand for national *policies* in education; local differences arising from different local expenditures are not as desirable as they may once have been. On the other hand, local *experiment* and *originality* need to be encouraged even more than they have been. To some extent a decline in local finance will discourage this, but the Regional Hospital Boards, although centrally financed, have been encouraged to be as diverse as possible, and the universities, which have proportionately more government money than the local authorities, have far greater freedom. One reason why they do so is because the Regional Hospital Boards and the University Grants Committee both contain representatives of the professions who operate the hospitals and the universities.

A monolithic Department would certainly be dangerous, not so much because of the danger of dictatorship as because of the dim conventionality of so many modern civil servants. One of the great myths of the English constitution which the recent past has swept away is the superiority of our Civil Service. It is, in fact, often short-sighted, self-satisfied, and stultifying, living to a quite extraordinary degree on memories of the war when, one feels, the Civil Service really lived life to the full. The Department of Education is still surrounded by blast walls and signs leading to A.R.P. points. A dim Department needs a counterpoise.

The best counterpoise would be the strength of the teachers and the influence of the parents. I have argued that both these forces are growing. If they can be organized they will replace the declining influence of the local authorities.

There are four problems to solve. The first is finance. This should come predominantly from the Government, which should collect the money for education as part of the total volume of national taxation.

Secondly, the education authorities must have a certain amount of autonomy – not too much, because most people want a national policy, but enough to encourage experiment, initiative, and responsibility. This means creating bodies that are big enough to be responsible, which suggests fairly big authorities. If local government could be radically reconstructed to create genuine large authorities it could be given its own taxing powers, but it seems most unlikely that this will happen in the near future.

Thirdly, the teachers must be far more closely involved in administration and policy than ever before, partly for better policy-making, and partly to raise their self-respect. This could be done by involving them in the running of the regional authorities, and the day-to-day running of the schools.

Fourthly, the parents must be involved in the affairs of the schools. Local Associations for the Advancement of State Education have come into existence all over the country, and these are forerunners of the sort of representative body which could really speak for the users of the education service, to whom far more attention will have to be paid than in the past. The degree to which parents have been bossed around by education officials is astonishing; although authorities like London have an exceptionally good record, some are hopelessly out of touch. 'You may want to know how the committee chooses a school for your child' said one leaflet about the 11 plus; it is not untypical – some places do not even issue leaflets. The freedom of choice guaranteed by statute has almost everywhere been denied.

What should be the form of the education authorities? There are really two questions here : One, the form the major authorities which decide the issues of policy should take. The other, what should be the form of the authorities near the schools themselves?

To the first, my answer is to create strong regional planning authorities for education, if possible directly elected, with strong teacher representation. The model for this is the Greater London Council and the other proposed Metropolitan Authorities. This would overcome the parochialism and inadequacy of the present smaller authorities. There is little doubt that only a big authority can provide special schools, a variety of secondary schools, and other services in sufficient qantities to enable realistic and adequate decisions to be taken about the satisfaction of the vastly diverse needs of the children. Little county boroughs may seem democratic, but the parents of an educationally sub-normal child merely see barriers, not democracy, when they cannot find a place for him in a good school. Such an alteration would bring a wind of change blowing through the places where major policies are made.

However, bigger authorities alone are not enough. Large-scale plans have to be implemented; the teachers must be involved. The introduction of a few more teachers at the regional level will still fail to lead to that real degree of mutual understanding which is necessary in, above all, the secondary schools. This is one of the jobs some schools' governing bodies were invented to perform but never do, largely because they are often without power and do not have teachers on them.

But a great many decisions need not be taken at Town Hall or County Hall level. They should be taken nearer the schools – appointments, some expenditure, the day-to-day administration of the schools. This is a field of the governing body. The answer to my second question would therefore be to enlarge and change the jobs of the governors.

Teachers in different types of school tend to be isolated from each others' problems. Moreover, governors too can be unaware of the problems of other schools in their district. There would therefore seem to be advantages in making governors responsible for more than one school. Indeed, a unit of 5,000 to 10,000 children may be needed to include a full range of a neighbourhood's schools. I would call this the School Group, and I would make it a joint committee of parents and teachers in the neighbourhood.

If the School Group had some of the major powers now exercised by the education authority, such as remodelling schools, re-equipping them, and re-allocating staff and pupils, then its members' conception of the interdependence of their schools would be more real. The corollary of this would be that the School Group would have to be of a size adequate to deal with most routine and some important questions, but at the same time small enough to be in continuous contact with a small number of schools. The second part of the solution to the problem of coordination would be to create panels of governors of each school or unit representatives, elected half by the teachers or their organizations in the School Group and half by the parents. The School Group would be given an annual budget, over which it would have virtually full control.

This is a way of developing a wider loyalty among teachers and parents than that given to the school alone. In this way the problems of transfer of pupils and staff which are essential to the working of a genuine policy of 'parity of esteem' can be discovered and overcome, and in this way the reluctance to be ordered about and experimented upon by 'local politicians' can be avoided.

The voluntary denominational schools would fit into this system, possibly more happily than at present, either by incorporation into a School Group, with the existing religious guarantees, or by the construction of a wholly sectarian School Group in areas where there is a close-knit religious community. So, too, would the 'independent' schools, as they are fitted into the public system. The objections to local political control advanced by these schools, which have some validity, cannot be maintained as strongly when professional teachers are half the controlling body. Any school with special reasons for remaining independent could be granted a position analogous to that of the teaching hospitals, directly under the Department.

There might be expected to flow from this policy a growth of professional responsibility, and greater experiment in organization and teaching. Emphasis would be shifted from the narrow independence of each individual school to the educational needs and possibilities of the whole local area. As a result, there could be an acceptance of the more valid parts of the case for the comprehensive school (at first within the limits imposed by existing buildings). At the very best, there could be greater flexibility and freedom in secondary education and a diminution of the importance of the break at the age of eleven, which is perhaps another way of expressing the first benefit.

What are the disadvantages of such a scheme – or, put another way, what are the advantages of the present system?

First, local autonomy is at present – to some extent, at least – guaranteed by the existence of local elected councils with independent sources of finance. These proposals will reduce their powers. Secondly, by putting finance almost wholly into the hands of the Department of Education, the powers of that body will be increased. Thirdly, in many areas the elevation of the school governors to an important administrative role as the local School Group will add another administrative layer to the structure of education.

These are serious objections which I believe can be answered. Local autonomy, for example, rests less on election and the rates than on the fact that councils can be trusted to do what they are set up to do. If they fail in their job neither the fact that they are elected nor that they levy rates will in the long run help them to survive. In particular, what guarantees freedom to take decisions without constant reference back to the Department is not how much money comes from it, but how far the authorities may be trusted to spend responsibly. This means that a regional authority which does not concern itself with day-to-day administration of the schools will be more likely to be effective than a number of small authorities are. In any case, if the teachers are involved in decisions this should make the day-to-day administration more effective.

Two other points are relevant: one is that the local 'freedom' desired is a freedom to experiment in education and not a freedom to vary standards (these are settled nationally). In other words, 'freedom' is to be judged (in part at least) by the freedom it gives the teachers. The other is that the 'independence' of local authorities derives in part (and probably in large part) from their elective nature – and this freedom is not abrogated by the proposals made here.

One further objection may be dealt with summarily. The panjandrums of English education believe that freedom inside the classroom is uniquely guaranteed by English local government. Experts in comparative education assure us that classroom habits are based on national traditions, and not on issues of local or state control. The best guarantee of freedom is a highly esteemed body of teachers – and in this respect England lags behind Scotland and other more distant countries.

Thus, in some senses, my financial proposals, and a growth in teacher representation, would represent an increase and not a diminution of local responsibility. In short, I have argued, first, for a substantial change in the structure of the education system, for a frank recognition of the role of the Department of Education, and for a considerable increase in its scope and power. In recent years the Secretary of State for Education has become one of the most important members of the Cabinet, in itself a welcome change. Secondly, I have argued for a much greater degree of professional self-government in order to raise the status of the teachers. Thirdly, I have argued for a system of central finance which alone could stand the enormous rate of growth and expenditure which must be envisaged.

The problem is to incorporate local interest and concern into this structure. Since almost all other local services have passed through a similar crisis in recent years and a number of them have been taken out of local hands, there seem to be strong arguments for a reconsideration of the place of local government in British life. It may well be, for instance, that we should move towards a series of powerful regional authorities responsible for health, planning, and the allocation of industry. What is certainly the case, however, is that the existing tendency to move education into the sphere of comparatively small local authorities is one which should be resisted.

All this is machinery. I have discussed it at length partly because I believe that the machinery of government is important, partly because it is what *can* be changed (whereas the spirit is said to move where it listeth), but mainly because in doing so I have been able to raise major questions.

Some of the present education authorities are too small to plan an effective education service. Some of them are too big to be in intimate day-to-day contact with the parents and teachers. None of them is really responsible to its local teachers and parents, however good a job it may be doing. We need to create an effective planning authority, with adequate units for research and development, which means a regional authority. But above all we need to involve parents and teachers in the day-to-day running of the schools.

If we want an education system which is adequate we need two things – more resources, and a more intimate concern to take account of the views of parents and teachers. These two are interdependent. A middle-class society spends more – much more – on education than a working-class one would; yet it also expects, as a condition of paying its bills, a concern for its wishes. Schools were *imposed* on the poor; they are *chosen* by the middle class. This is wholly to the good, but it means a change from the Poor Law attitude to the parents now adopted by so many authorities and head teachers.

Teachers need more self-government, too. In response to a request for training college and technical college lecturers to sit on the government bodies of their colleges, the leader of a great Labour-controlled council said, 'This council does not believe in syndicalism.' Indeed, while university teachers are almost completely self-governing, other school teachers are quite shocked to be asked whether they should have more say in their affairs or not; they cannot see that it has any connexion with their professional status. Those with rank may even oppose it. One woman principal of a training college in the West Country is openly indignant at any notion that 'her' staff might have a say in the affairs of 'her' college.

It surely must be self-evident that a true concern for vigorous local life in the schools and the colleges must mean more say for parents and more say for teachers. The questions are as urgent as any of the more obvious ones discussed earlier in this book if our schools are to be lively, independent places.

CHAPTER NINE

WHERE DO WE GO FROM HERE?

EDUCATION is full of schemes. Everybody has plans. Yet very few people look at it, as a whole, in the light of the needs of the times.

I have described a few of the changes in the economy and in society which are leading to a demand for a longer and more general education, and which could produce a body of people who are creative and independent, able to lead full and happy lives, and to earn their own livings and keep up with a rapidly changing society.

What is this growth of education for? It is necessary because the number of children is increasing. It is necessary because, as our society and the economy change, people have to be more resilient and more skilful. This means they have to have a broad general background on which to build a high degree of specialization. It is necessary for the happiness and welfare of the people.

But the customers of education have changed. We know far more than we used to about intelligence and ability, and the old-fashioned idealists have been proved to be right. Intelligence is not a fixed quantum : it grows in favourable circumstances. Therefore, as people become better off they tend to grow more capable; and, also, as the nation becomes richer it can afford more measures which develop the intelligence of its people.

A modern economy demands a great range of skills which offer far more opportunity to the average person to develop himself than ever before. The average parent now cares, too, about what sort of school his children go to. These two facts alone make opportunity for education a new and exciting prospect. But they change the terms of the debate. The problem is not now (as it once was) to identify the one clever child in a big group and rescue it; it is to give an adequate education to every child, especially those who are thought to be average or below average.

It so happens that the children who are neglected at present are precisely these – the average and the below-average. These are the children, too, who are mainly from the working class. So that the major task is to bring education adequate in quality and quantity to this group; and this means big changes.

To put it at its lowest, we need them if industry is not to run out of workers, for the more industry is provided with the right kind of workers, the more there is to spare for education. This is a fortunate concurrence. We need a more fluid economy to compete in Europe, and to cope with technological change; our ideal society is also more fluid and open – a static society has led to hardship and narrow-mindedness – and the economy and society together therefore need a far more flexible, open, and adequate education system. That is the equation.

This means more money. I have advocated that much more should be spent on education by raising new taxes, such as a tax on the employment of young people and skilled workers, and by nationalizing the education rate. This will raise the percentage of the national income spent on education from its present five and a half (compared with three and a half in 1955 and three at the end of the war) to seven per cent or so by 1975. Consequently education will loom much larger in future than it has in the past in national politics. The urgent task of finding enough finance for education implies a radical re-ordering of our social priorities.

This money needs to be spent at once on more teachers. These teachers will be needed to teach the extra children now being born (the birth-rate is higher than it was expected to be) and to teach more effectively those that we have already.

In particular, school-life needs to be longer (though the age of entry could be raised from five to six, with part-time attendance from the age of three made optional).

The schools the teachers teach in will change. Up to now, we have had separate kinds of school for separate kinds of child. The only justification for this separation is a pragmatic one – that the schools exist – not one based on acceptable knowledge of what children are like and what schools do to them. Consequently, the trend will be – and should be – towards a common secondary school, with the eradication of existing divisions between modern, grammar, and public schools. In particular this will do away with many of the problems of selection which now dog the primary schools, and the chances in life of so many children. We must develop a way of giving continuously new chances and second chances to all children and young people – and this means later and later selection.

All this depends on more teachers. 'More teachers' depends in turn on a much bigger system of higher education.

Universities at the top and the technical colleges at the bottom; too few places; over-specialization – these are the vices of higher education at the moment. We need many more places – and these must be provided in universities and colleges which are part of a more coherent and rational structure than at present. We need junior colleges to offer an alternative to the top of the sixth form and the first year of university, so that over-specialization at school can be avoided. We need new, experimental courses, a wide range of graduate schools. All this will cost money and will require careful planning. But an adequate higher education system is essential to any progress at all in education generally, and in society at large.

What of those who are not full-time students? Surely all young people from fifteen to twenty-one should still be regarded as the responsibility of the nation. Modern apprenticeships are, by and large, out of date and inefficient. Industrial training has been made a public responsibility; and all young people should have access to playing fields, common-rooms, and gymnasia which are at present available almost only to sixth-formers and students. If this is done, it seems to me that the need to raise the school-leaving age will become less urgent: it could be, after all, a matter of individual decision whether a boy or girl is better off at school, college, or working half-time in industry or business, provided there is a guarantee that formal education will still go on and that he or she is given the opportunity and incentive to develop outside the classroom and the factory. Of course, to do this, we should have to make earning less attractive (very heavy taxes on young people's earnings would help) and provide enough teachers.

The central issue is, of course, the teachers. To get the education system we need, we require 100,000 more teachers in the next ten years, and another 150,000 in the ten years after that. How shall we get them? First by expanding higher education; then, by raising salaries; above all, by raising the status of teaching. How to do this? Teaching has many handicaps. Teachers come mainly from the working class, the majority are women, and it is a rapidly expanding profession. High status in other jobs is associated with a middle-class background, a majority of men, and a limitation of entry – all courses closed to teaching. But self-government, the other great mark of a profession, is not; and it does seem that the advantages to education of a far greater degree of teacher participation in education would be a step forward to self-respect.

Self-respect is important because teaching has lagged behind in its self-criticism. Much of it is hopelessly out of date. If the best is to be got out of all the expensive resources that we think should be poured into the schools, we must begin a broad programme of improving teaching techniques of

116

using the latest knowledge and making full use of modern equipment and devices. In other words, we need better techniques and new ideas in teaching.

Not only teachers but parents are involved in this change. This generation has seen the growth of a zest for education in ordinary people which was previously typical only of the middle-class and of exceptional working-class families. Consequently the shortage of places and absence of choice in the public sector of education, which has always existed, is now felt more and more bitterly by more and more people. Yet parents are too often treated as people on the dole used to be treated – queue up and be grateful for what authority provides. Teachers and parents together will have to have far more say in how to run the schools.

This means a new structure of administration – a more adequate regional organization and a far more powerful organization of parents and teachers at a basic level, near the schools. This will help to keep up concern and interest in what the schools do.

All this is, in a sense, machinery. It is none the less important for that. Education is one way – possibly the major way – in which we can try to pull Britain into the modern age. To do that we have to pay for it.

I will end this book on a severely practical note. We need more education; we shall have to recruit 100,000 extra teachers in a decade; this will cost at least £100 million a year, cumulatively, which will increase our taxes. (In the note at the end of the book I have stated a few of the details taken from a recent N.I.E.S.R. book.)

The reasons why I have advocated all this are clear. Like all practising teachers, I am keen that my children should be brought up in a relaxed and happy atmosphere and that they should be well taught – but no better taught than the rest of their generation.

A NOTE ON COSTS AND TEACHERS

In case the bill seems too big, perhaps we should look back thirty, forty, and sixty years.

Think of the state of education in 1906, 1926, 1936, and now, and it is surprising how rapidly change has occurred.

In 1906 children were in classes of 80 or more. Only one child in 200 went on to a secondary school. Most children went to work at thirteen. The teachers for the most part were ex-pupil teachers, who had to teach from the age of thirteen or fourteen while they themselves finished their very limited secondary education. Many were completely untrained. A third to a half of the children were lousy and verminous, and enormous numbers were chronically diseased and under-nourished. Most schools had primitive sanitation, ill-lit class-rooms, no games, and a little 'drill'. The parents of many children were barely literate. The number of working-class children at universities could have been accommodated in one smallish hall. This is only sixty years ago. Many male old-age pensioners started school in a system in which those con-ditions prevailed.

Twenty years later a great deal had changed. The leaving age had been raised to fourteen. The secondary (grammar) schools had been invented by Morant and named by Coun-cillor Muggeridge and poor children got scholarsips. Health and nutrition were improving. The pupil-teaching system was ending. The universities had grown and graduates were coming into the schools. The Fisher Education Act of 1918, although its finance was then to be savagely attacked by Geddes and May (on the grounds that 'the education pro-vided by the State was often superior to that offered to the middle-class child'), provided a framework in which

educational provision could grow to meet the rapidly changing needs of the twenties and thirties. It did grow – slightly.

In 1936 the school-leaving age was about to be raised to
fifteen. Classes were smaller than they had been. The untrained teacher was on the way out. But the inadequacies of
the system were appalling. The fall in the number of children
born in the great slump meant that conditions could be
rapidly improved; but what opportunities were missed!
Teachers were often unemployed in the 1930s, while children
were taught in classes of fifty. Only about 6,000 ex-
elementary school boys and girls were at the universities;
hardly any at Oxford and Cambridge. Such were the realities
of capitalist economics.

Now, nearly thirty years later, the inadequacies are still
there. They are far fewer, though they seem bigger because
our sights have been raised. There have never been so many
good students, teachers, schools, and universities as there are
now; and all the signs are that this will be true in most years
for the foreseeable future.

We live in a time when education is booming. It took just
over one per cent of the national income in 1900: less than
three per cent in 1938; now it takes nearly six per cent.
There are nearly 400,000 teachers of all sorts in England and
Wales. Three and a half million new school-places have been
created since the war.

These facts suggest that there is one important point. In
the *short term*, education is short of resources. In the *long
run*, it need not be. In education it is no longer so much
going to be a matter of deciding where scarce resources
should be best concentrated, so that if the clever are to be
adequately taught other children cannot be. By the year
1990 at the latest the national income will be double what it
is now. Education expenditure will be more than double –
that is to say we could have 700,000 teachers instead of
370,000; we could double higher education places again from

the 450,000 or so we have in 1970. All children could be taught in small classes and stay at school until they want to leave at seventeen or eighteen.

There are, of course, limitations. For example, the child population could grow. This means that more teachers might be needed each year because of population growth alone.

Nevertheless in the long run we can probably do it. But it is a big job. Here are some figures taken from N.I.E.S.R. – some very conservative estimates of numbers of teachers needed to staff the schools in 1975.

In 1960 there were 340,000 teachers in England and Wales
By 1975 we may need as a minimum:

to staff classes where pupils stay on after fifteen	80,000 more
to reduce the size of the primary classes and provide nursery schools	125,000 more
to reduce the size of secondary classes	50,000 more
to provide new places in special schools	3,000 more
	about 600,000 teachers

To this must be added many more teachers in universities, colleges of education, and technical colleges. The nursery school expansion could probably be met by raising the minimum age of entry to school. By 1980 we will probably need 150,000 more teachers than in 1970. All this will cost *at least* an extra £100 million each year, cumulatively.

More about Penguins

Penguinews, which appears every month, contains details of all the new books issued by Penguins as they are published. From time to time it is supplemented by *Penguins in Print*, which is a complete list of all books published by Penguins which are in print. (There are well over three thousand of these.)

A specimen copy of *Penguinews* will be sent to you free on request, and you can become a subscriber for the price of the postage. For a year's issues (including the complete lists) please send 30p if you live in the United Kingdom, or 60p if you live elsewhere. Just write to Dept EP, Penguin Books Ltd, Harmondsworth, Middlesex, enclosing a cheque or postal order, and your name will be added to the mailing list.

Some other books published by Penguins are described on the following pages.

Note: *Penguinews* and *Penguins in Print* are not available in the U.S.A. or Canada

EDUCATION

W. O. *Lester Smith*

Intended for the general reader, this book attempts to provide an account of modern trends in educational theory
and practice, and it reviews current problems.

It presents for the reader's consideration most of the fundamental issues under discussion today in educational
circles – aims and principles, the interaction of home and
school, the curriculum, the significance of the neighbourhood, problems of control and administration, equality of
opportunity, the education and status of teachers, the
organization of secondary education, the influence of the
Churches and voluntary societies, and the educational needs
of an industrial society.

A brief survey of this kind can be a dreary catalogue if
it is not selective, and for that reason there are some important omissions. It has been assumed that many readers
will wish to study more closely aspects and issues that particularly interest them, and throughout there are references
to relevant literature, including many books to which the
author is specially indebted. A reading list has also been
appended in the hope that it will prove helpful. Several
revisions have been made in this reprint, to bring the book
up to date.

Also available by the same author

GOVERNMENT OF EDUCATION

SOVIET EDUCATION

Nigel Grant

Interest in Soviet education has intensified recently, due to an increasing public awareness of educational problems in general. There has, however, so far been a lack of a short, up-to-date, comprehensive account of the Russian educational system.

In this study Nigel Grant not only describes the different types of schools and colleges in the U.S.S.R., and the work they do, but also examines the educational system as a whole against its geographical, historical, social, and political background. As well as giving a very vivid impression of life in Soviet schools, he provides much fascinating material for comparison with our own educational theories and problems.

The author is a lecturer on educational theory at Jordanhill College of Education in Scotland.

A GUIDE TO ENGLISH SCHOOLS

Tyrrell Burgess

Only defence claims more from the nation's budget than education. Conscious that 'children get a better chance nowadays', more and more parents feel an increasing need to explore all the possibilities that exist for schooling.

This new book by Tyrrell Burgess provides a straightforward guide to schools of all kinds in England and Wales, together with an outline of their administration and structure. Nursery schools, primary schools, secondary modern and grammar schools are all factually described, as well as the preparatory and public schools of the private domain. In addition the author summarizes the facilities for further and higher education.

Parents – particularly of children approaching the age of five – will find this book a useful map of a territory where such signposts as 'multilateral' and 'direct-grant' tend to confuse the most eager explorer.

THE COMPREHENSIVE SCHOOL

REVISED EDITION

Robin Pedley

Britain's educational system will soon be based firmly on the comprehensive school, and in this new edition of an already successful Pelican the Director of the Exeter University Institute of Education gives a clear and critical picture of the comprehensive as it operates in England and Wales today. Professor Pedley first describes just what the 11+ is and does. Then, after dispelling the bogey that comprehensive schools need at least two thousand pupils in order to function, he goes on to demonstrate, by statistics, that those in existence are already rivalling the tripartite system in academic achievements. Finally, and most important, he argues that a good comprehensive school can both focus and mirror a community as can no other school.

Of all our educational establishments the comprehensive school is the least understood. This book, which contains a glossary of educational terms and a summary of country-wide plans for reorganization, offers to interested readers – especially parents – all the facts.

ENGLISH PROGRESSIVE SCHOOLS

Robert Skidelsky

The progressive schools – Abbotsholme, Dartington Hall, Bedales, Gordonstoun, Summerhill and others – seem to owe their public fame more to notoriety than to serious study of their educational aims. Yet, within the scholastic world, they have exercised a decisive influence on educational policies both in Europe and the United States.

A modern historian makes a thorough examination in this Pelican of the ideas which have motivated the English Progressive School movement in this century, of what they are genuinely trying to achieve and the difficulties they met. Taking the lives and writings of three of the principal pioneers – Cecil Reddie, A. S. Neill, and Kurt Hahn – he places their educational innovations in the historical and social context within which they have worked.

On one level Robert Skidelsky's book is a history of educational ideas; on another, an outline of the cultural setting which has brought partial acceptance : but above all – and this gives it direct human appeal – it is a sympathetic portrait of three extraordinary men.

THE UNIVERSITIES

V. H. H. Green

The universities have always played a vital role in British society, but in the last fifty years their importance has increased as dramatically as their numbers. The resulting changes – and the need to understand them – have been very much in Dr Green's mind in writing this book.

His text provides a much-needed short history of the 'stone' universities – Scottish as well as English – from their medieval foundations to the present day : but he has concentrated equally on the development of the 'red-brick' and 'plate-glass' universities and on the present role of university education as a whole in British society.

By relating the present system to its history and to social conditions Dr Green has shed light both on the present and past relevance of Britain's universities to her overall development.